Miserere

John Ricciardi

© 2025 Giovanni (John) Ricciardi

All rights reserved.

No part of this publication may be reproduced, distributed, or transmitted in any form or by any means, including photocopying, recording, or other electronic or mechanical methods, without the prior written permission of the publisher, except in the case of brief quotations embodied in critical reviews and certain other noncommercial uses permitted by copyright law.

Published by Donahue Publishing

First Edition

ISBN: 979-8-89864-028-6

For information about special discounts for bulk purchases, please contact Donahue Publishing at info@donahuepublishing.co.

www.donahuepublishing.co

Dedication

It is with great pleasure that I dedicate this copy of Miserere to you. I am delighted to share my odyssey in the literary world with you. May the narrative of these pages light a spark, stir your heart, and above all remind you that your story matters too.

May these pages invite you to look closer, think deeper, and remind you that power does not come with logic. History is written not only by the victors, but also by the eccentrics. Eccentricity is not a flaw, but a signal of madness and unchecked power.

This book is written to confirm your suspicions, deepen your confusion, and offer comfort in the fact that nobody really knows what to do, especially those in charge.

This book is for the curious, the skeptics, the bold, and the unhinged.

Thank you for reading between the lines.

Table of Contents

Introduction 1
Chapter 1 Miserere/Misericordia 3
Chapter 2 Unrests and Revolutions 13
Chapter 3 Revolutionaries 24
Chapter 4 Regimes that Collapsed 38
Chapter 5 Hypocrisy 47
Chapter 6 Xenophobia 54
Chapter 7 Megalomania/Narcissism 65
Chapter 8 Caprices of the Leaders 72
Chapter 9 Greed/Utopianism/Pseudonym 84
Chapter 10 Conspiracy Theories 96
Chapter 11 World 1968 Protests 114
Chapter 12 Influencers 141
Chapter 13 Leaders as Influencers 154
Chapter 14 Literary Artists 160
Chapter 15 Entertainment Artists 166
Chapter 16 Dreamers 171
Conclusion 176
Epilogue 179

Introduction

It was March 31, 2021, the day I decided that it was enough, and retired after dedicating 50 years to the electrical consulting engineering industry. I worked as an independent contractor for 40 of those 50 years, during which time I met thousands of culturally different individuals. Many of them held uncanny views on political, economic, and religious topics and manifested hostility when reminded that we are living in a multicultural and multiethnic democratic country. They seemed unwilling to be cautious about expressing ideas that did not apply universally. I will talk and elaborate on these types of individual behaviors throughout the chapters.

On the first day of retirement, not being a sportsman, I was faced with the dilemma of how to use my spare time. Then one day, while listening to Spotify, I came across some significant song compositions from the past that made me reflect on how these lyrics could, and still can, impact individual behavior today, particularly among world leaders.

Five compositions struck me profoundly enough that I convinced myself to write this book. These songs are "Miserere," composed by Gregorio Allegri in 1638, "Imagine" by John Lennon in 1971, "What's Going On" by Marvin Gaye in 1972, "One Love" by Bob Marley in 1977, and "Quattro amici al bar" (Four Friends at the Bar) by Gino Paoli in 1991.

In later chapters I will explore these five compositions in depth.

John Ricciardi

I decided to call this book *Miserere* because I attribute this Latin word to many of today's world leaders and all those individuals who utopistically think they are a step ahead of everybody else and are convinced, or more accurately persuaded by conspiracy theories, that they can change the world for the better.

Miserere and misericordia to those who still believe.

Chapter 1
Miserere/Misericordia

Miserere is a Latin word meaning "have mercy" and/or "have pity".

Misericordia is an Italian word meaning "have pity" and or "have compassion".

Both these words are very prominent during ritual performances in catholic churches. While most often heard in liturgical settings, these terms carry a broader meaning, a plea for mercy, pity, and compassion that extends beyond church walls.

Both *miserere* and *misericordia* are associated with catholic worship, and thus part of the biblical text used by many Christians. A musical/lyric setting was composed for the church called "*Miserere mei deus*" (Have mercy on me, God).

"*Miserere mei deus*" was composed by Gregorio Allegri in 1638, a singer/priest of the Sistine Chapel choir, to be sung exclusively within the Sistine Chapel walls during the holy week. *Miserere* is today regarded as one of the most beautiful pieces of music ever written.

Miserere was commissioned by Pope Urban VIII for the exclusive use in the Sistine Chapel during the *Tenebrae services* of the holy week (a solemn ceremony). It was so well composed that due to its extraordinary beauty, Pope Urban VIII forbade any transcription, publication, or performance outside of the Sistine Chapel. This prohibition lasted over 130 years.

Thanks to the great talent of Wolfgang Mozart, who, at the young age of 14, attended the performance of *Miserere* with his father in the Vatican and was able to transcribe the entire piece from memory. Therefore, today we can all enjoy this beautiful masterpiece composed by Gregorio Allegri.

There are many versions of *Miserere* today being sung. I love the Italian version sung by Pavarotti, Zucchero, and Bocelli.

On May 8, 2025, Cardinal Robert Francis Prevost of Chicago was elected 267th Pope of the Catholic Church to succeed Pope Francis (Jorge Mario Bergoglio).

Cardinal Robert Francis Prevost chose Leone (Leo) XIV as his pontiff's name.

Like many of his predecessors, the first speech from the window of St. Peter Basilica looking into the large crowd that filled St. Peter Square was simple and timeless: "Brothers and sisters, I send you greetings of peace to you, your families, and to all people of the world. May peace and love be with you all."

Given all the conflicts that presently exist throughout the world, whether political, bellicose, trade, or other forms of unrest, one wonders if any of these conflicts would induce leaders of the world to stand silently and reflect on the Pope's phrase. I think not. And so I use the words "*miserere* and *misericordia.*"

- *Miserere* to all those who are imposing their power and oppressing others.

- *Misericordia* to all those who are helpless through no fault of their own.

During one of my trips back to my birthplace, called Castelmauro, sipping a delightful cup of espresso with the local parson of the beautiful Renaissance-style church, he asked my thoughts on what the world has turned into. I simply answered that the cause of it was the "caprices" of the world leaders on any given day. The siblings of caprices afflicting all those leaders who, once they reach their untouchable throne of power, emanate all their behavior in forms of xenophobia, hypocrisy, megalomania, utopianism, and will do anything possible to create a legacy that will be remembered for many years after their death.

I will talk about leaders and their eccentric behavior in the following chapters of this book.

One may wonder how and why leaders of the catholic church, who had an enormous impact worldwide, have not prevented bellicose conflicts that continue in various parts of the world.

The Church's Paradox: Preaching Peace While War Persists

While Popes consistently profess love and peace, the Catholic Church has had a complex relationship with war throughout history. The Church has ranged from direct involvement that sometimes contributed to conflict, to acting as a powerful force for mediation and peace.

The 19th century saw significant tension between the Catholic Church and emerging states across Europe. This led to culture wars over issues like education, marriage, and the role of religion in public life:

1. ***Kulturkampf* in Prussia** – Otto Von Bismarck's government sought to neutralize Catholicism as a political force, leading to this cultural struggle.
2. ***Italian unification*** – The church under Pope Pius IX opposed Italian nationalism and the liberal movements seeking unification.

Throughout history, the catholic church and the popes have had a complex and significant impact on bellicose conflicts, oscillating between instigation, justification, mediation, and sometimes, direct participation.

The Church's impact on warfare can be understood through several key roles:

1. Mobilizing and justifying warfare:

Crusades: Perhaps the most direct and well-known example of papal influence on warfare is the Crusades. Beginning in the late 11th century, Popes, most famously Urban II, called for armed pilgrimages to the Holy Land to reclaim Jerusalem from Muslim rule. They mobilized secular rulers and knights by offering spiritual incentives like indulgences (remission of sins) for participation. These campaigns, while having complex motivations, were explicitly initiated, supported, and at times directed by the papacy, significantly increasing its power and prestige.

Defining "Just War": The Church developed the "Just War Theory", primarily shaped by figures like St. Augustine and St. Thomas Aquinas. This theological framework outlined conditions under which warfare could be considered morally permissible. While intended to limit violence and promote peace, it also provided moral justification for certain conflicts, particularly those deemed defensive or against "enemies of the Church" (such as heretics or infidels).

Against Heresy and Opponents: Popes also launched Crusades and sanctioned military actions against Christian groups deemed heretical (such as the Albigesian Crusade) and against political opponents of papal authority. This demonstrates the Church's willingness to use military force to enforce its doctrinal and political will.

2. **Direct military power:**

Military Religious Orders: The Church established and supported military religious orders (such as Knights Templar and Hospitallers). These orders were unique in that their members were both monks and knights, dedicated to fighting the Church's enemies and defending Christian interests. They provided the Church with a disciplined fighting force.

Papal States: The Popes directly ruled significant territories in Italy known as the Papal States. They maintained their own armies and engaged in conflicts to protect and expand these temporal possessions, acting much like any other secular ruler.

3. **Mediation and peace:**

"Truce of God" and "Peace of God": In the medieval period, the Church attempted to limit endemic warfare among Christian lords through movements like "Peace of God" (protecting non-combatants and Church property) and the "Truce of God" (prohibiting fighting on certain days of the week). While their effectiveness varied, they represent an effort by the Church to curb violence.

Diplomatic interventions: Throughout history, Popes have engaged in diplomatic efforts to mediate conflicts, negotiate peace treaties, and prevent wars. For instance, Pope Benedict XV proposed a Peace Plan during World War I, and later Popes like John Paul II played significant roles in advocating for peace and human rights.

Stance in the modern era: In the modern era, particularly following the devastation of World Wars, the Church has increasingly emphasized a presumption against the use of force, while still maintaining the Just War tradition as a last resort. Popes have strongly condemned the destructiveness of modern weaponry and advocated for disarmament and the peaceful resolution of disputes.

4. **Complexities and contradictions:**

Political pragmatism: Throughout history, the Church's involvement in conflicts was not always solely driven by religious motives. Popes often acted as political players, seeking to maintain or expand their influence in Europe. For example, during the Thirty Years' War, while nominally a religious conflict, Papal policies were often guided by a desire to maintain a balance of power, even at times aligning with Protestant forces against the Catholic Habsburgs if it served their political interests.

Internal division: The Church itself was not always a monolithic entity. There were internal disagreements and varying interpretations of theological principles, which could also impact its stance on conflicts.

The church and the Popes wielded immense power, both spiritual and temporal, which profoundly shaped the nature and course of bellicose conflicts. They could instigate wars, provide moral justification for violence, directly participate with their own forces, and also act as crucial mediators for peace. This multifaceted engagement reveals the complexity of the Church's role in human conflict.

5. The church's role in modern conflicts:

In World War I, Pope Benedict XV attempted to mediate peace by issuing a 1917 peace proposal, which was largely ignored.

In World War II, Pope Pius XII was criticized and defended for his diplomatic silence on the Holocaust.

In the Cold War and anti-communism, the Church, under Pope John Paul II, played a pivotal role in undermining communist regimes, particularly in Poland.

In modern conflicts, Popes Paul VI, John Paul II, Benedict XVI, and Francis have constantly condemned wars, nuclear arms, and the arms trade.

6. Modern Papal Influence

While popes have preached peace, some Church institutions have been accused of complicity in violence. Though the Church's influence has waned, its symbolic power remains significant. Papal inaugural addresses are broadcast worldwide and attended by heads of state, diplomats, and religious leaders. Popes, through the Vatican's authority, can influence public opinion, propose the Vatican as a venue for negotiation, and shift the conversation from geopolitics to shared humanity.

This influence may be subtle, but in the context of global diplomacy, it can be powerful. Some papal messages for peace and justice have been very influential, resulting in positive breakthroughs:

- Pope Francis helped facilitate the US-Cuba diplomatic thaw in 2014.
- Pope John Paul II was crucial in emboldening the anti-communist movement in Poland in 1978.
- In 2016, Pope Francis supported the Colombian government and the Revolutionary Armed Forces of Colombia to reach a peace deal.
- In 2019, Pope Francis urged the South Sudanese leaders to maintain peace.
- Papal addresses to the United Nations have influenced global discourse on human rights, disarmament, and poverty. These speeches are often referenced at international summits.

So it still puzzles me to see some of today's world leaders ignoring papal messages.

Songs of mercy were never meant to comfort the powerful. They were meant to disturb them. *Miserere* is not a hymn for the broken; it is a summons to the unbroken to break open their silence.

Miserere and Misericordia to those who still believe that sorrow is weakness.

John Ricciardi

And so, let there be mercy and grace for all who seek it. Mercy to the deserving, and even more to those who are not.

Chapter 2
Unrests and Revolutions

Karl Marx, with the collaboration of Friedrich Engels, published in 1848 the revolutionary political pamphlet called "Communist Manifesto," which lays out the theory of historical materialism, critiques capitalism, and calls for the working class (proletariat) to rise against the capitalist class (bourgeoisie).

It was written during political upheaval and industrial transformation in Europe and was published in London just before the 1848 revolutions that swept across Europe.

The revolutions were sparked by:

- Political unrest
- Political repression
- Economic hardship
- Social inequality
- Nationalist aspirations
- Ideological momentum
- And erupted in more than 50 countries:
- France
- Germany
- Austria
- Hungary
- Italy

- Denmark
- Netherlands

The theories of the Manifesto defined communism and its goals, including the abolition of private property, progressive income tax, free public education, and calls for global workers' solidarity and the end of child labor. The manifesto influenced later conflicts, revolutions, and the rise of revolutionaries. Major conflicts that followed were:

- Crimean War (1853-1856) Russia vs the Ottoman Empire, Britain, and France.
- American Civil War (1861) Union vs Confederacy.
- The Franco-Prussian War (1870-1871) led to German unification.
- World War I (1914-1918); global conflict that reshaped Europe and colonial empires. World War II (1939-1945) Axis vs Allies led to the Cold War and decolonization.
- The Korean War (1950-1953), the first Cold War conflict.
- Vietnam War (1955-1975), communist North vs US-backed South.
- Soviet Afghan War (1979-1989) Soviet forces vs Afghan mujahedin.
- Gulf War (1991) coalition forces vs Iraq.
- Iraq War (2003-2011), US-led invasion.

- Yugoslav Wars (1991-2001), ethnic conflicts after the breakup of Yugoslavia.

Major revolutions and uprisings that followed were:

- Paris Commune (France 1871)
- Russian Revolution (Russia 1917)
- Chinese Communist Revolution (China 1949)
- Cuban Revolution (Cuba 1959)
- Iranian Revolution (Iran 1979)
- Eastern Bloc Revolutions (1989, Poland, Hungary)
- Collapse of the Soviet Union (USSR 1991)
- Arab Spring (2011) Tunisia, Egypt, Syria

The revolutionaries who were influenced by the manifesto were:

- Vladimir Lenin (Russia), leader of the Bolshevik Revolution.
- Leon Trotsky (Russia), Marxist theorist and revolutionary.
- Mao Zedong (China), founder of the People's Republic of China.
- Che Guevara (Argentina), an iconic Marxist revolutionary.
- Fidel Castro (Cuba), leader of the Cuban Revolution.

- Ho Chi Minh (Vietnam), the Vietnamese president and revolutionary.
- Subcomandante Marcos (Mexico), leader of the Zapatista movement.
- Pol Pot (Cambodia) led the Khmer Rouge and ruled from 1975 to 1979.
- Muammar Gaddafi (Libya) seized power through a coup.
- Kim Il-Sung (North Korea) founded North Korea after the Japanese occupation.

Marx's ideology also continues to have a great impact on modern political movements, shaping everything from labor rights to global justice campaigns. Many political parties around the world have drawn directly from Marxist theories to advocate wealth redistribution, public ownership, and worker empowerment.

More theories and ideologies were written and adopted throughout the world following Marx's manifesto. Here is how revolutionary ideologies, especially those that shaped major movements and conflicts such as "Marxism-Leninism", "Maoism", and "Anarchism", all had a profound impact globally.

1. **Marxism-Leninism: Vladimir Lenin**

    - Based on Marx's theories, this movement developed, advocating a vanguard party to lead the working class to revolution.

- Believed in a two-stage revolution: socialism first, and stateless communism later.
- Emphasizes democratic centralism with internal debates followed by unified actions.
- Subsequently, Joseph Stalin formalized Marxism-Leninism in the USSR, adding centralized control and rapid industrialization.
- Became the dominant ideology in Eastern Europe, China, Cuba, Vietnam, and North Korea, generating variants like Titoism, Guevarism, and Ho Chi Minh Thought.
- Marxism-Leninism is still the official ideology in China, Cuba, Laos, and Vietnam, and has evolved into market socialism and is criticized for authoritarianism and repression, but praised for social equity and anti-imperialism.

2. **Maoism:**

- Developed by Mao Zedong in China, adapting Marxism-Leninism to an agrarian society.
- Emphasized peasant-led revolution and protracted people's war.
- Advocated continuous revolution to prevent capitalist restoration.
- The Great Leap Forward (1958-1962) was a disastrous attempt at industrialization.

- Cultural Revolution (1966-1976), where mass mobilization occurred, and elements of the bourgeois were purged.
- Inspired movements in Nepal, India, Peru, and the Philippines.
- China retains Maoist symbolism but has shifted toward pragmatic governance.
- Maoism remains influential in anti-globalization, environmental, and anti-capitalism theories.

3. **Anarchism:**

- Rejects all forms of hierarchical authority.
- Advocates voluntary cooperation, mutual aid, and direct democracy.
- Anarcho-communism, anarcho-syndicalism, and individualist anarchism form diverse schools of thought.
- Influenced by medieval philosophies such as Taoism (living in harmony), cynicism (skepticism of power), and stoicism (focusing on internal virtue).
- Major movements sparked by anarchism are the Spanish Civil War (1936 - 1939) in Catalonia.
- Paris Commune (1871). An early experiment.
- Influenced the Zapatista movement.
- Very active in climate justice, anti-authoritarian, and digital privacy movements.

- Thrives in grassroots activism.

While these ideologies are still adopted in countries like China, Vietnam, Cuba, Laos, and North Korea, these countries now favor economic pragmatism and geopolitical flexibility over doctrinaire purity.

Many of these countries today retain ideological frameworks rooted in Marxism-Leninism or Maoism, but their practical application has changed significantly for strategic, political, and particularly economic reasons.

There are many reasons why the efficacy of these ideologies has diminished.

- Globalization pressure (open markets, foreign investments, and trade deals demanding economic reforms).
- Technological changes (central planning struggling to keep pace with the digital economy and innovation).
- Public demands (general public expectations have increased drastically for political freedom and consumer choice).
- Internal contradictions (today, applying revolutionary ideologies in modern contexts can lead to inefficiencies and backlash).

A perfect example is China, which promotes Marxist values in education and party rhetoric but operates a vast market economy with billion-dollar tech firms.

Some revolutions were successful (Cuba, 1959), where workers were united under a strong leadership provided by Fidel Castro and Che Guevara.

Some other revolutions failed, such as the Hungarian Revolution of 1956, where a popular uprising against Soviet control lacked international support and was crushed by Soviet military intervention.

Some other revolutions had mixed results, such as the Arab Spring of 2010 to 2011, which sparked massive protests across the Middle East, where some regimes fell, such as Tunisia, and some others descended into chaos, like Libya and Syria.

Even where a successful uprising occurred (Cuba), in the long term, it could not sustain the change that the revolution brought due to challenges in institution-building. Creating stable governance institutions, economic reform to address inequality and poverty, and legitimacy through gaining public trust and international recognition proved difficult. Revolutions often burn hot and bright, fueled by passion and radical vision, but sustaining that momentum long-term is a different beast entirely.

What has begun as a liberation can morph into authoritarian stagnation and disillusionment.

Miserere

This is why revolutionary success often fizzles:

- Idealism vs reality, utopian visions rarely survive the complexity of political reality.
- Revolutionary leaders must transition from tearing down to building up (very difficult to achieve, not easy).
- Many movements dismantle old systems without having sustainable new ones ready.
- Fragile situations can collapse under pressure and sometimes can become corrupt.
- Expectations, during revolutions, are sometimes very exuberant and utopian.
- The general public (citizens) are not patient and may feel betrayed when changes do not match the initial promise.
- External forces like foreign powers, global markets, and sanctions can destabilize post-revolution governments.

Although Marx's ideas inspired massive social experiments across the 20th century, from the Soviet Union to Maoist China, Cuba, Vietnam, Laos, and beyond, the implementation of those ideologies often diverged from actual theories.

Here, I want to point out why many Marxist-inspired regimes struggled:

- Authoritarianism vs democracy: Marx envisioned a classless and stateless society, but many regimes

became centralized and authoritarian. Dissent was often crushed, contradicting ideals of liberation.
- Economic inefficiencies: Centralized planning systems often stifled innovation and mismanaged resources. Shortages, poor quality goods, and black markets popped up in egalitarian economies.
- Power struggle: Revolutionary parties promised rule by the proletariat, but leadership often became a new elite, far from the classes Marx imagined.
- Cultural oversimplification: Marx underestimated how deeply culture, religion, nationalism, and history shape societies. And when applying rigid frameworks, it sometimes did not resonate with the local context.
- Global capitalist pressure: Many socialist countries faced isolation, sanctions, and conflicts from capitalist nations, hence complicating their development.

Marx's famous phrase, "The philosophers have only interpreted the world in various ways; the point, however, is to change it," but changing it turned out to be far more complex.

Marx's critique of capitalism remains widely studied in wealth inequality, ecological collapse, and labor exploitation persistence.

Some modern thinkers who have tried to reimagine Marx's theories are:

- **Slavoj Žižek** — Slovenian philosopher, neo-Marxist who embraces contradictions, failure, and incompleteness as inherent to nature and society.
- **Chantal Mouffe** — Belgian University professor and political theorist who argues that democracy thrives on conflict, not just consensus.
- **Yanis Varoufakis** — Greek economist and politician, argues that we have moved from capitalism to techno-feudalism.

How long will these new ideologies that these modern thinkers are offering last before others come to the surface and history repeats?

Miserere and Misericordia to the fires that burned for change and the hands that smothered them.

And so, let there be mercy and grace for all who seek it. Mercy to the deserving, and even more to those who are not.

John Ricciardi

Chapter 3
Revolutionaries

In Chapter 2, I briefly talked about notorious world revolutionaries. In this chapter, I am elaborating on those revolutionaries and their influence on global political movements.

1. **Leon Trotsky**
    - Inspired the Trotskyist movement worldwide, including anti-globalization. He argued that socialist revolutions must be international.
    - Founded a global network of revolutionary socialist parties.

2. **Che Guevara**
    - Developed tactics that influenced insurgencies in Latin America, Africa, and Asia.
    - Became an icon for the anti-capitalism youth movement.
    - Inspired leaders like Subcomandante Marcos and movements like the Mexican students of 1968.

3. **Ho Chi Minh**
    - Inspired liberation movements in Africa and Latin America.
    - Modeled how anticolonial struggle could align with socialist ideology.

4. **Josep Tito**
    - Advocated for socialism independent of Soviet control.
    - Influenced post-colonial states seeking autonomy.

5. **Fidel Castro**
    - Sparked leftist movements across Latin America and Africa.
    - Challenged U.S. hegemony and supported global revolutionary movements.
    - His emphasis on education and healthcare influenced progressive policies worldwide.

6. **Subcomandante Marcos**
    - Advocated indigenous rights, anti-neoliberalism, and participatory democracy.
    - Used symbolism and digital media to mobilize global solidarity.

7. **Meena Keshwar Kamal**
    - Founded Afghanistan's first independent women's rights movement.
    - Linked class struggle with gender liberation.
    - Her movement continues to inspire feminist resistance in Afghanistan and beyond.

8. **Sun Yat-Sen**
- Pioneered democratic ideals in China and influenced Taiwan's political development.
- Shaped modern Chinese nationalism and inspired reformist movements.

Che Guevara and other revolutionaries not listed above have left a profound global imprint that transcends their immediate political contexts.

He championed Marxist socialism and fiercely opposed US imperialism, inspiring leftist movements.

He envisioned a society driven by moral values and collective good rather than material wealth. His theory argued that small, committed revolutionary groups could ignite mass uprisings.

After helping Castro to lead the Cuban Revolution, Guevara attempted to export revolution to Congo and Bolivia. His image and writings fueled student protests in Europe, liberation struggles in Africa, and uprisings in Latin America.

Although other icon revolutionaries like Che are listed as influencers, I want to elaborate more on Che Guevara, who was the most globally influential revolutionary.

Che Guevara was an Argentinian Marxist revolutionary who did not find space, despite sharing some theories, within Juan Domingo Perón's administration in Argentina.

Che was a military theorist and guerrilla leader. His style had become a ubiquitous symbol of rebellion. As a medical student, Guevara travelled throughout South America and was appalled by the poverty, hunger, and disease he witnessed. His desire to help overturn what he saw as the capitalist exploitation of Latin America by the United States prompted his involvement in Guatemala's social reforms under President Jacobo Árbenz, whose eventual overthrow solidified Guevara's political ideology.

Later in Mexico, he met the Castro brothers (Raúl and Fidel) and joined the July 26th Movement and sailed to Cuba. After the Cuban Revolution, Guevara played key roles in the new government, like reviewing the appeals and death sentences for those convicted as war criminals, instituting agrarian land reform, helping spearhead a nationwide literacy campaign, and traversing the globe as a diplomat on behalf of Cuban socialism. The same position allowed him to play a central role in training the militia forces who repelled the Bay of Pigs invasion and bringing Soviet nuclear-armed ballistic missiles to Cuba, which preceded the 1962 Cuban Missile Crisis.

His experiences and study of Marxism-Leninism led him to posit that the Third World's underdevelopment and dependence was an intrinsic result of imperialism, neocolonialism, and monopoly capitalism, with the only remedies being proletarian internationalism and world revolution. He left Cuba to foment continental revolutions across Africa and South America unsuccessfully and was captured by the CIA, who were assisted by Bolivian forces, and executed.

Other world revolutionaries were:

9. Mahatma Gandhi

- Indian lawyer, anti-colonial nationalist, and spiritual leader.
- Led the Indian independence movement against British rule.
- Gandhi had a profound impact on the world, advocating for equality and freedom that earned him the place as one of history's most influential figures.
- His principles of non-violence and peaceful resistance continue to inspire social and political change.

10. Nelson Mandela

- Anti apartheid revolutionary and politician. He dedicated his life to fighting against racial segregation and inequality under the apartheid regime.
- After spending 27 years in prison, he emerged as a symbol of resistance and reconciliation, advocating for peaceful transition and national unity.
- His commitment to justice and equality earned him global admiration and a Nobel Peace Prize.
- His legacy as a revolutionary peacemaker continues to inspire movements for social justice and human rights.

11. Patrick Lumumba

- A Congolese independence leader and the first Prime Minister of the Democratic Republic of the Congo.
- Lumumba played a pivotal role in the struggle for independence from Belgian colonial rule, but his time in power was short-lived as political turmoil and external interference led to his overthrow and tragic assassination in 1961.
- His legacy as a revolutionary and martyr remains a symbol of African independence and the fight against colonialism.

12. George Washington

- An American revolutionary leader and the first president of the United States.
- Washington's willingness to relinquish power after his presidency set a precedent for the peaceful transfer of power and solidified his status as one of the founding fathers of the nation.

13. Ho Chi Minh

- A Vietnamese revolutionary and the founding father of the Democratic Republic of Vietnam.
- He led the resistance against French colonization and later against the United States during the Vietnam War.

- Ho Chi Minh's leadership and vision continue to shape Vietnam and inspire movements for independence and self-determination.

14. James Connolly

- An Irish socialist revolutionary who, along with other rebels, sought to establish an independent Irish Republic to end British rule.
- His commitment to worker rights, Irish nationalism, and the pursuit of social justice made him a beloved figure among Irish republicans.
- He was executed following the failed uprising. His impact on the fight for Irish independence remains deeply influential in Irish history and politics.

15. Joseph Stalin

- His economic and social policies transformed the Soviet Union into a major world power.
- His rule was marked by widespread purges, forced collectivization, and political repression that led to the suffering and death of millions.
- His authoritarian leadership and brutal regime left a controversial legacy for Soviet history and the global political landscape.

16. Pol Pot

- He implemented radical policies that aimed to create an agrarian communist society, resulting in widespread forced labor, mass executions, and the infamous Cambodian genocide. His brutal regime caused the deaths of millions of Cambodians.
- Pol Pot's reign of terror stands as a chilling reminder of the atrocities committed in the name of revolution, leaving a legacy of horror and suffering.

17. Bhagat Singh

- An Indian revolutionary and a prominent figure in the Indian independence movement against British colonial rule.
- He advocated for armed resistance and played a significant role in several acts of revolutionary violence against the British government.
- Singh's martyrdom at the hands of the British authorities in 1931 left an indelible mark on the fight for independence and inspired generations of Indians in their struggle for freedom.

18. Emiliano Zapata

- A Mexican revolutionary leader and a key figure in the Mexican Revolution.

- He was a champion of agrarian reform and the rights of peasants and indigenous communities.
- He led the liberation army of the South, advocating for land redistribution and social justice.
- His slogan "Land and Liberty" symbolized his commitment to the landless farmers and his fight against the oppressive regime of Porfirio Diaz.
- His revolutionary spirit and his legacy as a defender of the marginalized continue to inspire movements for social and economic equality in Mexico.

19. Ahmed Ben Bella

- An Algerian nationalist and the first president of Algeria after the country gained independence from France in 1962.
- He was a central figure in the National Liberation Front and led the armed struggle against French colonial rule.
- His presidency was marked by political challenges and internal conflicts, leading to his removal from power.
- His fight against colonialism remains an integral part of the country's history.

20. Rosa Luxemburg

- A Polish-German Marxist revolutionary and political theorist.
- She was a prominent figure in the German and international socialist movements, advocating for social and economic justice.
- Her critiques of capitalism, imperialism, and militarism resonated with many, and she actively fought for workers' rights and the establishment of a socialist society.
- Her unwavering commitment to revolutionary ideals, her intellectual contributions, and her fearless pursuit of justice made her a highly influential figure in socialist and feminist movements.

21. Enver Hoxha

- An Albanian communist politician and the leader of Albania from 1944 to 1985. Hoxha's rule was characterized by an isolationist and oppressive regime marked by purges, political repression, and complete severance of ties with the outside world.
- His rigid implementation of Stalinist principles led to the stifling of political dissent and suppression of freedom.
- Hoxha's authoritarian leadership left Albania in a state of deep isolation and underdevelopment for decades.

22. Kwame Nkrumah

- A Ghanaian nationalist who led the Gold Coast to independence from British colonial rule in 1957.
- He became Prime Minister and later President of Ghana.
- He was a champion of Pan-Africanism and advocated for the unity and liberation of African nations.
- As a revolutionary leader and for his contributions to African unity, his legacy continues to shape the narrative of African history and inspire new generations.
- His vision for a united and prosperous Africa made him a prominent figure in the decolonization movement and an inspiration for independence movements across Africa.

23. Emperor Meiji

- A Japanese monarch and a pivotal figure in Japan's Meiji Restoration.
- His ascension to the throne marked the end of the feudal era and the beginning of Japan's rapid modernization and westernization.
- Under his leadership, Japan underwent significant political, social, and economic reforms, propelling it into a major world power.

- His determined vision to modernize Japan laid the foundation for its transformation into a modern nation-state and set the stage for its future success on the global stage.

These courageous revolutionaries from all corners of the globe, each with their own unique stories and struggles, are fueled by a burning desire to break free from the shackles of tyranny, discrimination, and injustice. From political leaders to freedom fighters, thinkers, and activists, these revolutionaries paved the way for change by challenging oppressive systems, demanding equal rights, and fighting to reshape the course of their nations and the world.

From the battlefields of independence wars to the podiums of influential speeches, their legacy continues to inspire generations to stand up, speak out, and strive for a better tomorrow.

The impact of these revolutionaries on today's world is profound and multifaceted, shaping modern political thought, international relations, and movements for social justice.

Their inspiration travels from non-violent resistance and democratic movements to influencing authoritarian regimes and contributing to violent conflicts.

- Nonviolent resistance, social justice, civil disobedience, and peaceful protest have had a lasting impact on movements for human rights around the globe.

- Communism and state control profoundly impacted global politics by establishing or inspiring communist states. Their actions led to the rise of one-party rule, state-controlled economies, and significant human rights abuses.
- Nationalist and anti-colonial movements. This type of revolutionary was driven by the desire for national liberation from colonial rule, highlighting resistance against foreign intervention, challenges, and dangers of post-colonialism and misalignment with superpowers.
- Radical ideologies and violence did not bode well with some of these revolutionaries' ideologies that have gone wrong.

Some of these revolutionaries' ideologies also impact current world leaders, socially, politically, and culturally.

- Ideological influence to legitimize policies or inspire national unity.
- Calls for justice and reforms, advocating system change through democratic reform.
- Symbol storytelling and populist narratives by giving emotional weight to speeches and adopting revolutionary language to frame themselves as outsiders battling corrupt elites.
- Soft power inspiration, promoting revolutionary history to attract allies through shared legacy.
- Resistance movements in global discourse.

- Grassroots connection by emulating revolutionary tactics.
- Human rights agenda by adopting policies rooted in equity and civil liberties.

Although Gandhi and Che were both revolutionaries, their paths to their movements were totally diverse.

◊ **Gandhi:**
- Nonviolence and truth force ideologies inspired Martin Luther King Jr., Nelson Mandela, the Dalai Lama, Al Gore, Cesar Chavez, Steve Jobs, and the UK and Germany.

◊ **Che:**
- Armed resistance and radical change influenced Latin America (Bolivia, Nicaragua, Colombia), Africa (Congo, Algeria), and Europe (France and Italy).
- Pop culture with his iconic image of the beret.
- Activists inspired by Che were Evo Morales, Rigoberta Menchú, Subcomandante Marcos, Hugo Chávez, and the Sandinistas.

Miserere and Misericordia to the dreamers who dared and the systems that devoured them.

And so, let there be mercy and grace for all who seek it. Mercy to the deserving, and even more to those who are not.

John Ricciardi

Chapter 4
Regimes that Collapsed

Many regimes have come and gone since the 1948 revolutions in Europe and after the publication of Karl Marx's communist manifesto.

Many regimes that were inspired by Marxist principles and attempted to implement the same ultimately collapsed or transformed due to internal contradictions, economic failures, or political resistance. There have been other failed regimes that did not adopt Marxist ideology but also collapsed.

Major Marxist-inspired regimes that failed were:

- Soviet Union (1922-1991)
- East Germany (1949-1990)
- Yugoslavia (1945-1992)
- Cambodia (1975-1979) Khmer Rouge regime
- Ethiopia (1974-1991) Derg regime
- Afghanistan (1978-1992)

The regimes failed due to economic mismanagement (economies struggled with inefficiency, lack of innovation, and poor resource allocation); political repression (many regimes suppressed dissent, leading to unrest and resistance); neglect of political institutions (many regimes underestimated the role of political institutions and overemphasized economic determinism); failure to adapt (these regimes failed to evolve with global changes, remaining rigid with ideology).

Some countries have successfully blended socialist principles with democracy, called "democratic socialism", adopting multi-party democracy, a mixed economy with regulated capitalism, allowing limited property, public and private ownership, and gradual reform through elections. These countries that successfully blended socialism with a democratic framework are:

1. **Sweden**
   - Universal healthcare and education
   - Strong labor protection
   - Thriving capitalist economy with high taxes and redistribution
2. **Denmark**
   - Wealth from oil is invested in public welfare.
   - Free education and health care
   - High standard of living and strong democratic institutions
3. **Germany**
   - Robust welfare system
   - Worker co-determination in corporate governance
   - Strong unions and a social market economy
4. **Norway**
   - Wealth from oil invested in public welfare

- Free education and healthcare
- High standard of living and strong democratic institutions

A major regime collapse of the 20th century was Argentina's Perón regime, which fell in 1955 due to economic decline (inflation, stagnation, and declining exports), conflict with the Church, authoritarianism, and a military coup. Unlike Marxist regimes that collapsed under systematic economic failure, Perón's downfall was more about political mismanagement and elite opposition than ideological rigidity.

Juan Domingo Perón, although he did not adopt Marxist ideology, borrowed selectively from socialist and labor-oriented ideas. He called his movement "Peronism," which was distinct from Marxism, positioning itself against both capitalism and communism, calling it the "third position".

There were similarities with Marxist ideas, such as:

- **Pro-labor** (supporting labor unions, worker rights, social security, and welfare).
- **Redistribution policies** (state intervention in the economy, nationalized key industries, reduced poverty and inequality).
- **Class focus** (social justice, giving political power to the working class).

Yet Perón diverged from Marxism in crucial ways:

- **Anti-communism** (suppressed Marxist parties and leftist dissidents).

Perón's goal was unity under a strong state, not revolution.

Che Guevara, a committed Marxist-Leninist revolutionary, observed Perón's social reforms but saw him as someone who used the working class for political power, calling Peronism "bourgeois nationalism" and rejecting Perón's third position.

Perón was overthrown in 1955 in a military coup called "Revolución Libertadora". His fall was the result of mixed political, social, religious, and economic tensions that had been building throughout his presidency.

He governed in an authoritarian manner, censored the press, suppressed political opposition, and cracked down on dissent. The labor unions were controlled by the regime, and critics were silenced or imprisoned.

He clashed with the Catholic hierarchy, legalized divorce and prostitution, removed religious education from schools, and even banned religious processions.

In the early 1950s, Argentina's economy started to deteriorate:

- Falling exports
- Rising inflation
- Budget deficit
- Foreign currency shortage
- Inefficient industries

- Unprofitable industries
- Growing discontent of classes
- The death of Evita

Nationalism and Catholicism (aligned himself with the Catholic Church), and cooperation between classes.

In September 1955, a full-blown revolt by army and Navy officers succeeded in forcing Perón into exile.

Peronism still remains a powerful force in Argentine politics. A movement that includes left-leaning and right-leaning factions, its emphasis on social justice, national sovereignty, and labor rights continues to resonate.

Like the Peronism regime, other non-Marxist-inspired regimes collapsed throughout history. These failures span ideologies, including fascism, monarchism, and military dictatorship.

1. **Fascist Italy (1922-1943)**

    - Overthrown during World War II after military defeats and internal dissent.
    - Benito Mussolini, the leader of fascist Italy, promoted ideologies of ultra nationalist, authoritarian, and anti-communist policies coupled with militarism and suppression of dissent that backfired during a national crisis.

2. Nazi Germany (1933-1945)

- Defeated in World War II.
- Adolf Hitler, the leader of Nazi ideology, promoted totalitarian, racist, and expansionist policies.
- Hitler's appointment as chancellor in 1933, through the "Reichstag Fire Decree" and the Enabling Act, obtained dictatorial powers and banned all other parties, making the Nazi Party the sole legal party.

3. Imperial Russia (up to 1917)

- Tsar Nicholas II, the leader, was overthrown in the Bolshevik Revolution.
- His ideology of absolute monarchy with rigid class hierarchy led to ignoring social unrest and resisting reform that triggered revolutionary upheaval.

4. Shah of Iran (1941-1979)

- Overthrown in the Islamic Revolution.
- Mohammad Reza Pahlavi, the leader, promoted the ideology of a secular monarchy with Western alignment.
- A 1979 referendum established an Islamic Republic, resulting in the ratification of a new Constitution.

5. Military dictatorships in Latin America

- Chile's Augusto Pinochet ruled from 1973 to 1990, and came to power leading a military coup on September 11, 1973, overthrowing the democratically elected socialist president Allende and bringing a military dictatorship with neo liberal economic reforms and harsh repression of dissent. In a 1988 plebiscite, voters rejected Pinochet's continued rule, leading to a democratic election in 1989.
- Brazil had numerous military dictatorship presidents who ruled Brazil from 1964 to 1985. A military coup on March 31, 1964, ousted President João Goulart and established a military regime of authoritarian rule with censorship, torture, and economic modernization. Brazil's repression peaked under Medici with widespread torture and suppression of civil liberties, leading to gradual liberalization under Geisel and Figueiredo. A civilian was elected president in 1985.
- Argentina's military Junta had multiple rulers from 1976 to 1983. In March 1976, a military coup removed Isabel Perón, establishing a military dictatorship of brutal rule focused on purging those deemed subversive, a category that included anyone opposing the regime. Argentina's repression

was the most brutal, with systematic disappearances and clandestine detention centers. The military defeat in the Falklands War in 1982 led to the collapse of the regime, and elections were held in 1983.

Another regime, the Japanese monarchy, although it did not collapse, underwent a dramatic transformation from imperial autocracy to a symbol constitutional monarchy. Japan became a modern imperial state, expanding aggressively across Asia. After Japan's surrender in 1945 following atomic bombing and military defeat, a new political order emerged.

In the 1947 Constitution, Japan redefined the emperor's role to become a symbol of the state and unity of the people rather than a ruler. Although the monarchy survived, its absolute power was abolished, and the emperor remains only a ceremonial figure.

Japan, Germany, and other monarchies that remain have adapted by adopting modern values, with ceremonial roles, media engagement, and cultural preservation.

So, across history, regimes have collapsed or transformed through the actions of revolutionary individuals or mass movements. Yet, despite centuries of lessons, today's leaders still engage in conflicts (military, ideological, economic, cultural, religious) with a stubbornness that feels almost timeless. Despite historical lessons, these conflicts persist for various motives:

1. **Addiction to power**

    - Moral clarity and power control are often obscured by fear of loss and political survival.

2. **Nationalism and identity**

    - Economic interests over resources, markets, arms industries, and geopolitical competition incentivize conflicts.
    - Institutional inertia makes it very difficult to dismantle systems built on conflict easily. Failure to internalize history occurs when leaders pick historical narratives to justify current actions.

It seems that each generation of leaders must restudy and relearn the cost of arrogance, the fragility of peace, and the danger of unchecked power.

Miserere and Misericordia to the ruins that once promised salvation.

And so, let there be mercy and grace for all who seek it. Mercy to the deserving, and even more to those who are not.

Chapter 5
Hypocrisy

Through the years, I have many times encountered individuals at the office or coffee bars who manifested dislike of the city and country's system they lived in, admiring the communist regime systems while crucifying capitalism vigorously, yet they continue to enjoy the freedoms and benefits that the capitalist system offers.

These individuals are frustrated with their lives, blaming the democracies in which they live while publicly admiring the economic systems of the communist regimes (particularly those of Russia and China).

How hypocritical and contradictory can this be when Western liberalism is criticized and authoritarian and state control are praised? The most hypocritical evidence is the communist regime. Before examining communist hypocrisy in depth, let me elaborate on hypocrisy itself. The most classical and used form of hypocrisy is "do as I say, not as I do".

Feigned virtue, double standards, biases, self-awareness, and mostly self-interest.

The general hypocrisy can be described briefly as follows:

- People experience discomfort when their behavior is inconsistent, thus changing their behavior, beliefs, and reducing their inconsistency.
- Because there is a tendency in human beings to always attribute success to internal factors and failures to external ones, it makes it easier to be hypocritical without acknowledging it.
- There is also a strong tendency to pay particular attention to information supporting those beliefs (conspiracy theories, which will be discussed in another chapter).
- Individuals may be unaware of their inconsistencies, not being coherent between the words and their actions.
- The thirst in humans to demonstrate and manifest their knowledge to others, craving acceptance and approval, thus exposing themselves to being perceived as having either an inferior or a superiority complex.

All the above forms of hypocrisy can cause trust erosion, preventing the formation of meaningful relationships, questioning the validity of principles, loss of credibility and reputation, and impeding progress, where hypocritical behavior can generate anger and resentment, contributing to conflicts. The most transparent sign of hypocrisy is very evident in politics and religion.

Communist hypocrisy is stark when examined closely. The ideology's stated goals are equality, collective ownership, and worker empowerment. Yet the reality reveals a farce.

The stock exchange symbolizes the Western world's capitalism.

China and Russia are also adopting the stock market system (in Shanghai and Moscow) to raise capital, attract foreign investment, drive economic growth, modernize financial systems, and compete globally.

The Shanghai stock exchange was founded in the 19th century by foreign traders and banks, becoming the financial hub of East Asia. It was shut down after the communist revolution in 1949.

Russia, in St. Petersburg, in the early 20th century had a very successful stock market which closed during World War I, permanently in 1917 after the Bolshevik Revolution.

In 1848, Karl Marx, with the collaboration of Friedrich Engels, published the "Communist Manifesto," which called, amongst other things, for the working class to rise against capitalism.

Lenin (Russia) and Mao (China), who firmly believed in Marx's theories, adopted the manifesto policies and formed the "USSR", the Union of Soviet Socialist Republics, and "PRC", the People's Republic of China, respectively.

After decades of adopting policies outlined in the manifesto, both regimes woke up and realized that the policies did not work. They mostly saw their economies falling well behind the Western (capitalistic) world. Thus, by early 1990, both countries reopened their respective stock exchanges, while continuing to promote communism (classless society), denying to themselves the real reason that the system did not work and will not ever work. (How hypocritical can one be?)

The Shanghai stock exchange has become so important, becoming one of the world's largest, that in 2019, a NASDAQ-style exchange (SSE STAR) was launched to support the fast-developing tech innovation.

The Moscow stock exchange, which was formed through merger of other exchanges, going through privatization, instability, scandals and sanctions, is now recognized as a mature and successful exchange.

So it is acceptable to use capitalist systems to advance financial economic status, even if they do not fully embrace free market capitalism and are state-controlled and not of the free enterprise system. They use capitalist tools without following its ideology.

To best demonstrate leaders and public hypocrisy, here are some points I would like to highlight:

1. **Bellicose Conflicts:**

    Vladimir Putin, president of Russia, has reportedly condemned Israeli actions against Iran as "unprovoked and unjustified aggression", offering to mediate while Russia has been engaged in large-scale military conflicts in Ukraine for over three years. Russia yet maintains relationships in the Middle East. Condemning Israeli strikes on Iran allows Russia to position itself as a defender of state sovereignty and international law in that context, while aligning with Iran's interests and potentially undermining US influence. This behavior is inconsistent when viewed alongside its own actions in Ukraine. Russia cited security concerns and historical claims to justify its military operations, which are seen as a violation of Ukraine's sovereignty and territorial integrity. This double standard is seen by international bodies and nations, highlighted by critics accusing Russia of applying international laws to suit its geopolitical objectives. Although Russia's official statements call for de-escalation and diplomatic solutions in the Middle East, it continues its military operations in Ukraine.

2. Trade (tariffs) conflict:

Donald Trump, president of the United States of America, is advocating for "America first" (manufacturing in America), after the US has benefited significantly from decades of globalization, which involved shifting manufacturing to other countries for lower costs and access to global supply chains. The US has accumulated immense wealth through trade, lower consumer prices, and access to diverse markets, even though jobs were lost in some manufacturing sectors.

This represents a shift from a long-standing economic paradigm that the US championed, as it attempts to prioritize domestic jobs and industrial development over globalization, even if it comes at the cost of higher consumer prices and reduced trade volume.

3. **Global Solidarity:**

The killing in May 2020 of a black man by the name of George Floyd in Minneapolis, Minnesota, sparked outrage not only across the US but around the world. Many saw this as a moment to stand against racism and discrimination, provoking massive worldwide protests in big city squares. Although this may have been seen as a gesture of solidarity, the moral here is that other countries have their domestic racism issues, which are unsolved, needing to be addressed, and therefore these protests are more performative rather than meaningful and constructive. So before showing solidarity, people of other countries shall reflect on what is happening at home and examine their own structures.

Solidarity should start with self-awareness before calling out injustice elsewhere, and also confront biases in one's backyard.

What does true solidarity mean when injustice exists within our own borders?

Miserere

Miserere and Misericordia to the mouths that preach peace while feeding war.

And so, let there be mercy and grace for all who seek it. Mercy to the deserving, and even more to those who are not.

Chapter 6
Xenophobia

Often during social conversations at the coffee bar while sharing a cup of coffee with friends and acquaintances, somebody in the group would be contradicting and manifesting negativity, obstinately affirming their beliefs, showing behavior rooted in xenophobia, driven mostly by envy.

I say xenophobia derives in many individuals from envy, which is a negative emotion of discontent and resentment, generated by the desire for something others possess, or by wishing others to lack that same knowledge.

Sometimes it arises from social comparison, thus leading to feelings of inferiority or hostility.

Envy can be "benign envy" (which can motivate self-improvement and praise for others), or it can be "malicious envy" (the desire for others to fail).

1. The Psychology of Xenophobia

Xenophobia is the fear or dislike of anything perceived as foreign, manifesting in hostile attitudes, discrimination, and aggressive behavior towards people of other nationalities, ethnic groups, cultures, or those considered outsiders (sometimes those considered outsiders could be amongst friends just because they may be bashful, shy, and need a bit more time to respond).

When a group of outsiders is perceived to be successful or possess qualities that others lack, it can trigger envy among members, which can transform into xenophobia when envious feelings lead to resentment, hostility, and a desire to see the failure of the outsiders and place them in a disadvantaged position.

A resentment towards those who possess values or virtues that others desire but cannot achieve or are unable to attain similar success can lead to malicious envy, which rationalizes itself through xenophobic beliefs that disparage or dehumanize other groups.

Xenophobia can often be perceived as blaming outsiders for social problems such as economic hardship, social changes, or loss of jobs, driving people to believe that the outsider group's success is at the expense of the local in-group, leading to a desire to remove or diminish their influence. Underlying feelings of insecurity or inferiority within an individual or group can make them more prone to envy. When this envy is directed towards foreign or other groups, it can manifest as xenophobia as a way to project their own insecurities and maintain a sense of superiority.

2. Types and Triggers of Xenophobia

The main types of xenophobia are immigrant and cultural:

- Immigrant xenophobia is the dislike or fear of people perceived to be immigrants.
- Cultural xenophobia is the dislike or hostility toward different cultures.

Factors that might cause xenophobia, in addition to envy explained above, are motivated by:

- **Power** – Political leaders are known to use xenophobia as a tool to get votes, using outsiders as scapegoats for social problems that they promise to fix.
- **Insecurity** – When an individual or group feels that they have less access to resources or are in danger, they want someone to blame.
- Greed – During the gold rush, the US government displaced native Americans from their lands during the "Trail of Tears."
- **Prejudices** – Xenophobia can stem from racism, islamophobia, anti-Semitism, and other forms of oppression, which fuel xenophobia towards other groups.

Other factors that can contribute to xenophobic behavior are:

- Lack of diversity
- Education
- Fear of strangers
- Self-awareness

- Cultural appreciation
- Inclusivity
- Using privilege
- Speaking out
- Harassment

3. Xenophobia as Prejudice, Not Phobia

Xenophobia is the fear, hatred, distrust, and frustration directed toward anyone the dominant group in a society deems strange or foreign.

This, rather than being a phobia, is a form of prejudice and discrimination emanating mainly from those individuals who suffer from inferiority and superiority complexes and are so frustrated with their lives that they believe anything a social platform posts or any conspiracy theory promotes.

4. The American Paradox

The United States of America has a long history of immigration. In fact, many immigrants celebrate their origins and the idea of the United States as a "nation of immigrants". The United States, during the 20th century, remained the World's largest immigrant-receiving country, admitting more immigrants than any other country in the 21st century, yet the United States is also a nation of xenophobia.

Since 1892, the United States has deported more immigrants than any other nation. The US history, politics, and laws reveal a constant and enduring hostility toward immigrants.

Although xenophobia is a global phenomenon, there are distinct national, regional, and local differences.

American capitalism, American democracy, and American leadership, despite xenophobia, have been very successful and prosperously enviable (here we see another form of xenophobia—envy of America's global position).

Xenophobia in the United States has existed since white settler colonialism and slavery, becoming part of the systemic racism and other forms of bigotry and discrimination defining American society. It has adapted to and shaped successive migrations and settlements of people from around the world.

Although many immigrants were and are let into mostly Western countries, xenophobia allows these same countries to close the door at any given time in the service of capitalism. Xenophobia also means big business. The United States has arrested, detained, and deported a growing number of immigrants, relying on privately run immigrant detention centers to carry out these initiatives by instituting corporations such as "Corrections Corporation of America" (CCA).

Xenophobia and American capitalism work together, siphoning working-class resentment away from corporate greed and economic inequality and directing it toward immigrants, thus promoting and celebrating the "capitalist immigrant" that embodies the American work ethic, upholding popular beliefs in a meritocratic economy in both good and bad times. Americans have supported and fully participated in political xenophobia at the border to secure votes, elect anti-immigrant lawmakers, make anti-immigrant policies, and gain political power.

5. **Impact of Xenophobic Leaders:**

Here is a brief description of xenophobic leaders' rhetoric and policies of influential leaders like Donald Trump, Vladimir Putin, Benjamin Netanyahu, and Xi Jinping that have had wide-ranging consequences domestically and internationally.

◊ **Donald Trump**

- Trump's rhetoric correlated with a spike in hate crimes in US counties that hosted his rallies. His use of terms like "China virus" and "rapists" to describe immigrants fueled anti-Asian and anti-Latino sentiments.
- The immigration ban, also referred to as the "Muslim ban", targeted several Muslim-majority countries and was viewed as a clear act of religious and ethnic discrimination.

- "America first" nationalism promoted an isolationist foreign policy and blamed job loss on globalization.
- Trade wars alienated allies and undermined US soft power, the country's ability to influence other nations through attraction and persuasion rather than coercion.
- Trump's rhetoric and policies emboldened far-right and white nationalist groups while also sparking global concern about democratic backsliding and intolerance.

◊ **Vladimir Putin**

- Putin's mobilization policies disproportionally targeted ethnic minorities, leading to increased Xenophobia and racism within Russia. Migrants from Central Asia have faced harassment, violence, and deportation.
- "Russkiy Mir" (Russian world) promotes the Russian world within Russia and all Russian-speaking populations outside of Russia's borders, thus justifying interference in Ukraine, Georgia, etc.
- Anti-immigrant sentiment: Russia has seen regular state crackdowns on migrants from Central Asia and the Caucasus, framed in the media as threats to national stability.
- Anti-Western: Putin frames the West as culturally degenerate and threatening traditional Russian

values, fostering a siege mentality that emphasizes Russian uniqueness and moral superiority.
- Putin's use of nationalism to consolidate power and justify aggressive foreign policy often comes at the expense of minorities and migrant communities.

◊ **Benjamin Netanyahu**

- Nationalist stance and alignment with far-right ministers have contributed to the dehumanization of Palestinians and a breakdown in relations with diaspora Jews who feel alienated by his policies.
- The Nation State Law declared Israel the nation state of the Jewish people, downgrading Arabic's status and drawing criticism for marginalizing Palestinian citizens of Israel.
- Security rhetoric: He regularly frames Palestinians as an existential threat, contributing to systemic discrimination and military occupation.
- African migrants: He pushed for the deportation of African asylum seekers, calling them infiltrators and suggesting they pose a Jewish demographic threat to Israel's identity.
- Netanyahu's rejection of cease-fire proposals and expansionist policies has drawn international condemnation.

- Netanyahu's policies and rhetoric have been seen as deepening divisions between Jewish and non-Jewish citizens and contributing to human rights concerns in the occupied territories.

◊ **Xi Jinping**

- Xi's nationalist discourse during the COVID-19 pandemic framed foreigners as a threat, reinforcing a fortress China mentality and fueling xenophobia domestically.
- Xi's refusal to import foreign vaccines during COVID-19, despite domestic shortages, was driven by nationalist pride rather than public health concerns.
- Uyghur crackdown, massive human rights abuses in Xinjiang, including internment camps, forced labor, and efforts to erase Uyghur culture, language, and religion, have been labeled "cultural genocide".
- Han nationalism, the promotion of Han cultural dominance under the guise of "national unity", pressures ethnic minorities to assimilate through education, surveillance, and social controls.
- The Chinese Dream blends national pride with suspicion of Western values and foreign influences. Critics argue this fosters internal xenophobia and justifies repression.

- Xi's ethno-nationalist policies have caused global outrage over human rights abuses, especially in Xinjiang and Tibet, and contributed to a growing divide between China and liberal democracies.

6. The Pattern Across Borders

While differing in context and severity, all four leaders have strategically invoked xenophobia to consolidate political power and shape national identity. Whether through rhetoric, policy, or force, their approaches normalize the marginalization of minorities and deepen global trends of authoritarian nationalism. As Xenophobic discourse gains traction in powerful states, the consequences for democratic norms, human rights, and international relations grow more serious.

Xenophobia is the fear, hatred, and distrust of outsiders. It harms not only immigrants, but anyone that the dominant group in a society deems strange. It is not a phobia, in the medical sense, but a widespread form of prejudice and discrimination.

Xenophobia can be part of a political platform, the result of institutional policies, or a form of interpersonal abuse.

It negatively impacts the lives of many people globally and is often a cause of oppression.

Miserere and Misericordia to the borders drawn in blood and ignorance.

John Ricciardi

And so let there be mercy and grace for all who seek it.

Mercy to the deserving and even more to those who are not.

Chapter 7
Megalomania/Narcissism

As I described the symptoms of xenophobia of some individuals in the preceding chapter 6, at the bar drinking espresso, there were others showing symptoms of narcissism and megalomania behavior.

A friend who frequented the bar regularly would, before sitting down and ordering a coffee or drink, step into the men's room to ensure that his hair and outfit were all properly in position without any visible glitches. This is narcissism, a type of megalomania.

Berlusconi, the former Italian prime minister, besides displaying behavior of arrogance, was also full of personal vanity to the point where he had cosmetic surgeries and hair transplants.

Berlusconi's behavior was so arrogant that he was sometimes compared to Roman emperors and Popes. Known for his "Bunga Bunga" parties and his womanizing, which he seemed to view as part of his mythic status—a desirable, powerful man.

Defining Megalomania

Megalomania is a psychological condition characterized by delusions of grandeur, a belief in exceptional power, importance, or fame, an obsessive desire for control, often manifesting in dominating others or seeking unchecked authority, and seeing oneself as uniquely gifted, destined for greatness.

Megalomania is often considered a symptom of other disorders, such as narcissistic and paranoid personality disorders.

Megalomaniac and/or narcissistic behaviors can be seen as delusional obsessions with power and dominance, manifesting in extreme authoritarian or grandiose behavior in political leaders. Some historical leaders are often described as megalomaniacs:

1. **Adolf Hitler (Germany)** – Obsessed with racial purity. Belief in personal destiny in reshaping the world and totalitarian control.
2. **Joseph Stalin (Soviet Union)** – Cult of personality, belief in his infallibility, total state control.
3. **Benito Mussolini (Italy)** – Promoted himself as the embodiment of the Italian state, with delusional dreams of restoring the Roman Empire.
4. **Napoleon Bonaparte (France)** – Declared himself emperor, tried to conquer all of Europe.
5. **Mao Zedong (China)** – Personality cult, devastating social engineering, viewed himself as the sole guide to the country.
6. **Kim Il-Sung (North Korea)** – Extreme cult of personality, hereditary dictatorship, total control over citizens' lives.

7. **Vladimir Putin (Russia)** – Power consolidation, long-term rule, nationalism, belief in his historic mission to restore Russian influence.
8. **Saddam Hussein (Iraq)** – Cult of personality; brutal repression, portrait of himself as a historic Arab leader.
9. **Muammar Gaddafi (Libya)** – Published his own ideology (the Green Book), portrayed himself as the king of kings of Africa.
10. **Tayyip Erdogan (Turkey)** – Increasing authoritarianism, crackdown on dissent, shift from parliamentary to presidential system.
11. **Donald Trump (United States)** – Grandiosity, loyalty demands, attempted to overturn electoral loss, self-centered narrative.
12. **Xi Jinping (China)** – Elimination of term limits, consolidation of power, massive surveillance, and control.
13. **Nicolas Maduro (Venezuela)** – Clings to power despite economic collapse, suppresses opposition, and presents himself as the savior of socialism.

Notable Megalomaniac Leaders: Case Studies

Some of the most notable megalomaniac leaders of the past and present time:

4a. Joseph Stalin (Soviet Union) – Created a totalitarian regime with absolute control over political, social, and economic life. Saturated public space with his personality through statues and images. Orchestrated massive purges, eliminating anyone seen as a threat, including allies, and believed his leadership was essential for the survival of socialism, justifying massive repression and famine.

4b. Benito Mussolini (Italy) – Declared himself "Il Duce" (the leader) and centralized power, dreamed of reviving the Roman empire, started wars in Africa and Europe, orchestrated intense propaganda campaigns, glorifying his image and fascism, and believed that he could restore Italy's greatness.

4c. Donald Trump (United States) – Grandiose self-image, routinely describing himself as the best president, businessman, or negotiator. Demanded absolute loyalty from officials and viewed dissent as betrayal, undermining trust in the media, courts, intelligence agencies, and elections. He rejected the 2020 electoral defeat, promoted baseless claims of fraud, and incited supporters, culminating in the Capitol riot on January 6, 2021. He cast himself as the sole savior against corrupt elites, adoring and requiring constant public attention and validation through rallies, social media, and cable news.

While Donald Trump is not ruling as a dictator, many scholars, psychologists, and critics have pointed to narcissistic and authoritarian behavior, comparing it to early stages of megalomania-driven regimes.

4d. Vladimir Putin – Changed laws and the constitution to stay in power (maybe up to 2036), sees himself as the restorer of Russian greatness, often invoking imperial Soviet-era grandeur. Erasure of opposition threats (see Alexander Navalny) by jailing and poisoning. Annexation of Crimea and invasion of Ukraine (2022). He staged media events to show himself as a strongman and promote censorship and propaganda as a global force against the West.

Putin's behavior is a reflection of Russia's failure, compared to the Western world, to achieve economic success and stability, manifesting deep personal ambition and historic revisionism.

4e. Tayyip Erdogan (Turkey) – Transitioned Turkey from a parliamentary to a presidential system, increasing his authority. After a failed coup in 2016, he purged public servants, jailed journalists, and crushed civil society, increasing references to Erdogan as the sole protector of Turkey's values and independence. Presents himself as a modern-day sultan, invoking Ottoman history and labeling protesters traitors in his attempt to redefine the nation's identity.

Erdogan's style mirrors that of a classic megalomaniac leader, showing such extravagance as building a massive presidential palace (1100 rooms), symbolizing self-aggrandizement.

4f. Nicolas Maduro (Venezuela) – Claims a divine mission by speaking of his connection to the late Hugo Chavez in spiritual terms, denying reality by maintaining power amid hyperinflation, starvation, and mass emigration, insisting that the country is under siege by foreign enemies. Rigged elections, arrested political opponents, and shut down independent media. Created a parallel assembly to override the democratically elected legislature (constituent assembly). He blames the economic collapse on US sanctions and internal traitors, refusing accountability. Maduro shows classic megalomania in his detachment from national suffering, reliance on conspiracies and beliefs in his own righteousness despite widespread condemnation, and depiction of himself as a revolutionary hero.

The Roots: Paranoia

Both megalomania and narcissism derive from "paranoia", a process marked by irrational distrust or suspicion of others, ranging from mild unease to severe delusional beliefs that others are trying to harm, deceive, or exploit, which makes it difficult for them to trust others. Paranoia can be viewed as feeling constantly judged, watched, and conspired against, being hostile and defensive, holding grudges, and being unable to forgive.

Paranoia in megalomania could be seen as jealousy of others' greatness as measured by power, success, and achievement, leading to authoritarian behavior.

Paranoia in narcissism can be interpreted by vulnerable individuals as personal attacks, assuming others talk behind their backs, or feeling persecuted when their image is challenged.

Miserere and Misericordia to the thrones built on mirrors and madness.

Miserere

And so, let there be mercy and grace for all who seek it.

Mercy to the deserving, and even more to those who are not.

Chapter 8
Caprices of the Leaders

Sometimes, listening or reading about world leaders' behavior reminds me of my adolescent years in high school, where youngsters interacted capriciously to reach what they aimed for, thus manifesting a distinct childish behavior.

Adolescent Caprices

The childish behavior of adolescent caprices can be attributed to brain development, where the responsibility for decision making, impulse control, and therefore, possible consequences is still maturing during teenage years, which means that adolescents are more prone to act on impulse, misinterpret social cues, and engage in risky or irrational behavior. Teenagers also develop emotional skills with feelings that can be intense and can fluctuate rapidly, leading to melodramatic reactions and quick anger.

All these different types of behaviors are part of adolescence that sometimes can manifest in babyish interests reflecting their transition period.

These behaviors, although frustrating to parents and teachers, are a challenging part of development.

Adult Caprices

The childish behavior of adult caprices normally expresses emotional immaturity or an inability to control emotions that one can expect from a grown individual. Adults often consistently deflect responsibility by blaming others for their actions and problems, have very poor impulse control by acting first, and thinking later about consequences derived from reckless speaking and impolite interruptions. Another sign of adult childish behavior is individuals consistently seeking to be the center of attention by disregarding boundaries and aggressively name-calling when things do not go their way or their views are not shared.

In summary, childish caprices in both age groups lack a fully developed emotional cognitive regulation. While in adolescents it is a phase of development, in adults it signifies a delay in emotional maturity.

Adolescent caprices are often impulsive and emotional but have limited impact due to a lack of autonomy.

Adult caprices may be less impulsive on the surface, but are often more consequential after gaining power and experience.

Adolescents have the tendency to act on impulse, whim, and irrational desire, thus producing behavior that may appear erratic, dramatic, or rebellious.

In adulthood, capricious behavior can persist but is filtered through experience and social power. While adults' authority over others (professionally or as political leaders), their whims carry greater consequences. While adolescent caprice is a symptom of development, adult caprices are an action of unchecked power.

Here is the paradox: adult caprices are less visible but far more dangerous.

World Leaders and Their Whims

Having talked about adolescent and adult caprices, here are my thoughts on the current world leaders' whims, which may, directly or indirectly, cause us to pay dire consequences at some point.

◊ **Donald Trump**

- He reversed positions on issues like Ukraine and the Federal Reserve, contradicting his own past statements.
- His administration has deployed military forces domestically, proposing federal takeover of cities.
- His foreign policy has strained alliances and accelerated a shift towards a fragmented world order.
- His impulsive leadership leads to extreme extraversion, low emotional stability, and high narcissism.
- His sudden policy reversals or confrontational diplomacy reflected deep-seated personality traits rather than strategic calculations.

◊ **Vladimir Putin**

- His war in Ukraine has been marked by experts and critics as an erratic decision, including nuclear threats and internal purges.
- His rhetoric and actions reflect a desire to restore Russian dominance.
- His psychological profile shifted over time from cooperative to increasingly adversarial, leading to growing frustration and distrust, which contributed to impulsive decisions like the annexation of Crimea and the invasion of Ukraine.

◊ **Benjamin Netanyahu**

- His military actions in Syria and Gaza have alarmed even closer allies like the U.S., with him being named "a madman" and "a child who won't behave".
- His decisions are often seen as driven by internal pressure rather than strategic diplomacy.

◊ **Xi Jinping**

- He has consolidated power to an unprecedented degree, sidelining dissent and elevating national security above economic growth.
- He is reshaping international relations, challenging Western influence and promoting a state-centric worldview.

- While some countries view China as a rising superpower, others remain wary of its influence and governance.

◊ **Elon Musk**

- His political involvement, controversial statements, and creation of a new political party have raised concerns about his impact on democracy and corporate governance.
- His meetings with world leaders while holding government influence have sparked ethical debates.
- His ventures into AI companions and provocative social media posts have drawn criticism for promoting harmful stereotypes.

Theories of Power and Psychology

Having explored some world leaders' capricious behavior, which may impact their decision-making, the main attribution of this whim is the acquisition of power and being able to hold on to it. Their position of power may experience changes in their thinking and behavior.

There are some theories about how power afflicts an individual's psychology once the individual has achieved the position of high-level power:

1. **Theory of inhibition** – This theory posits that power triggers a behavioral approach system, leading individuals to be more goal-oriented and optimistic, which can

be either a positive trait or make the individual riskier, inappropriate, or unethical.

2. **Theory of reduced empathy** – Individuals, once they have achieved power, may become less attuned to the perspectives of others and increase social distance between themselves and their subordinates, devaluing the abilities of those with less power.

3. **Theory of cognitive biases** – Individuals are susceptible to cognitive issues, which can be amplified by their position. Confirmation bias can lead them to seek out and interpret information that confirms their pre-existing beliefs, while hindsight bias can make them believe they were right about a decision even when evidence suggests otherwise.

4. **Great man theory** – This theory of leadership proposes that certain individuals are born with innate qualities like charisma, confidence, and intelligence to be great leaders. This perspective influences the popular imagination of what a leader can be or is.

5. **Trait theories** – These theories suggest that certain personality traits are associated with effective leadership, but they also acknowledge that the same traits can lead to different outcomes.

6. **Theory of narcissism** – Some leaders may exhibit a high dominance orientation, seeking to assert control

over others. This type of collective narcissism ties their followers to the success and superiority of their group or nation.

Institutional Context

The role of the political system and the specific context in which leaders operate are also critical factors:

1. **Checks and balances** – In democratic systems with strong institutions and checks and balances, as opposed to systems with a cult of personality where the leader's image is carefully managed and glorified, leaders have either freer or more constrained ability to act.

2. **Public opinion and political survival** – Leaders must also consider their political survival. Sometimes, acting in a way that appears capricious may be a calculated move to appeal to a specific voter base or to appease powerful constituencies, such as the military or industrial backers.

Sometimes, what appears to be a whimsical or impulsive act may be a deliberate, though not necessarily rational, strategy.

A leader may act unpredictably to keep opponents off balance. An irrational or risky decision can be a way to signal strength to both domestic and international audiences.

Leaders can use vague and emotionally resonant slogans that allow supporters to project their own meanings onto them, thus creating strong affective bonds that transcend rational policy-making and allow the leader to act with a greater degree of flexibility.

Authoritarian vs. Democratic Systems

The leaders in authoritarian regimes are often perceived as more prone to capricious rule:

- **Kim Jong Un (North Korea)** – As supreme leader, he holds unchecked authority over all aspects of governance, with decisions often made without institutional checks.
- **Ali Khamenei (Iran)** – As the supreme leader, he wields ultimate religious and political power, and his decisions can override elected officials.
- **Vladimir Putin** – Though Russia has elections, critics argue that Putin's long tenure and control over media and institutions allow for highly personalized rule.
- **Mohammed Bin Salman (Saudi Arabia)** – As crown prince and prime minister, he has pushed rapid reforms and made sweeping decisions sometimes seen as impulsive.

In contrast, leaders in democratic systems are constrained by parliaments, courts, and public opinion, making capricious governance far less feasible. (Emmanuel Macron, France, Keir Starmer, UK, Justin Trudeau, Canada). Of course, even in democracies, moments of impulsive leadership can emerge, especially during a crisis or when leaders face little to no opposition. But the system tends to temper those instincts.

Consequences of Impulsive Leadership

Impulsive leadership can send shockwaves through global politics, sometimes with dramatic, unpredictable consequences:

1. **Policy Volatility** – Sudden reversals of established policies can destabilize international relations and confuse allies. Also, impulsive decisions often lack long-term planning, leading to inconsistent governance and poor implementation.

2. **Diplomatic tension** – Leaders may make rash statements or decisions that strain diplomatic ties or provoke adversaries. Unplanned alliances or confrontational moves can reshape global dynamics overnight.

3. **Erosion of trust** – Impulsive actions can frequently make leaders appear unreliable or erratic, weakening their credibility on the world stage. This unpredictability can cause civil unrest and loss of public support, domestically and internationally.

4. **Psychological impact** – Traits like narcissism, impulsivity, and lack of empathy can drive decisions that prioritize personal gains over collective welfare, which can lead to conflict escalation and breakdowns in multilateral cooperation.

5. **Electoral consequences** – Impulsive leadership can polarize electorates, leading to spontaneous voter turnout driven by emotion rather than policy, and it may also trigger resignations or leadership changes, disrupting political continuity.

Historical and Modern Examples

Some notorious historical and modern leaders with impulsive traits are listed below:

- **Alexander the Great** – Cut the Gordian knot with a sword. Led to rapid conquests.
- **Napoleon Bonaparte** – Invaded Russia in 1812 despite warnings, thus marking the decline of his empire.
- **Catherine the Great** – Overthrew her husband in a swift coup, becoming empress of Russia.
- **Vlad the Impaler** – Mass executions of boyars during Easter, cementing reputation for cruelty.
- **Grigori Rasputin** – Erratic political influence over Russian royalty. Contributed to revolutionary unrest.
- **Genghis Khan** – Abrupt tactical shifts during campaigns, secured victories, and built the largest land empire.
- **Elon Musk** – Abrupt decisions at Twitter (mass layoffs, policy shifts) created instability, lost advertisers, and damaged reputation.
- **Boris Johnson** – Sudden policy reversals during Brexit and COVID-19.

- **Donald Trump** – Unfiltered tweets and rapid executive orders, a polarized electorate, and strained international relations.
- **Jair Bolsonaro** – Spontaneous remarks and pandemic response, global criticism, and domestic unrest.
- **Volodymyr Zelenskyy** – Bold wartime decisions under pressure, seen as decisive and risky.

Understanding Capricious Leadership

The impulsive behavior in leadership can be a mix of personality, strategy, and circumstances. It can either project strength or spark chaos, inspire loyalty, or trigger backlash. Volatile unpredictability often lies in the leader's self-awareness, emotional regulation, and ability to balance impulse. The impulse behavior in modern leaders can deeply affect political stability and public perception:

- Political stability
- Frequent policy reversals
- Sudden resignations or firings
- Hastily formed alliances
- Unplanned legislation
- Public perception
- Unfiltered media statements
- Erratic behavior
- Rapid reactions in polling data
- Emotional decisions

Miserere

The idea that world leaders act on caprices has some merit. It is an understanding rooted in the complex interplay of individual psychology, personality traits, and the political and institutional context in which they operate, though some behaviors may truly be impulsive, while others might be part of a calculated strategy, rooted in deeply held beliefs, or a consequence of power.

Caprices refer to a sudden, unpredictable change in mood, behavior, or decisions, often driven by whim rather than reason.

Whims, impulses, ego, desire, and mood are all psychological dimensions that can drive an individual toward caprices.

Caprices can be perceived as an expression of freedom, authenticity, and individual desire, sometimes as eccentric, as in artists, inventors, and visionaries who can be misunderstood, leading to confusion and misunderstanding.

Miserere and Misericordia to the whims that shape destinies without care.

And so, let there be mercy and grace for all who seek it.

Mercy to the deserving, and even more to those who are not.

John Ricciardi

Chapter 9
Greed/Utopianism/Pseudonym

In previous chapters, I discussed the most common behavioral adjectives suitable for today's world leaders; however, there are other behavioral interpretations that can be addressed, such as "greed, utopianism, and pseudonym". While these three concepts are related, there is no perfect way to equate the three subjects. A person who dreams of living in a perfect society has a utopian vision that may eliminate excessive desire for more than is needed. On the other hand, someone acting out of greed and pursuing a utopian vision can be seen as a pseudo-idealist.

Sometimes, these concepts interact in a contradictory way, as the concept of pseudonym can be applied to today's world leaders in ways that can motivate or shape the direction of political systems.

1. **Greed:**

    Personal gain, while not always visible, accusations of personal greed are common. Leaders may be accused of using their power to enrich themselves, their families, and their allies through corruption, kickbacks, or favorable business dealings, manifesting an insatiable thirst for wealth.

Beyond money, greed can be a lust for power itself. Leaders may be driven by an intense desire to hold and expand their influence, sometimes at the expense of democratic processes or the well-being of their citizens, which can lead to authoritarian tendencies. The suppression of dissent and a refusal to cede power, even when required constitutionally.

Leaders may justify policies that benefit a small elite, arguing that this will ultimately create wealth for everyone, even if it exacerbates inequality.

2. **Utopianism:**

Leaders often use utopian language to rally support, promising a better tomorrow, a great nation, or a perfect society. This can be a powerful motivator for voters, but it can also be a dangerous tool if the leader is unwilling to compromise.

Some leaders are genuinely motivated by a deeply held utopian vision, inducing positive changes, such as fighting for social justice or environmental protection, however a rigid utopian ideology can also be dangerous, leading to suppression of individual rights, persecution of those who do not fit the ideal, and the disregard for real world, consequences in pursuit of a perfect but ultimately unattainable goal.

Modern politics is often a struggle between a leader's utopian promises and the messy reality of governance. A leader may promise to eliminate poverty but face economic constraints. They may (and will) promise a perfectly just society, but face a complex legal system and deep-seated social issues. The gap between the utopian ideal and the political reality can lead to public disillusionment.

3. **Pseudonym:**

Leaders may use pseudonyms as a deception tool, taking the form of state-sponsored propaganda where a leader's actions are presented under a different name. It can also involve the use of fake social media accounts or anonymous sources to spread disinformation and attack opponents.

The concept of a pseudonym can be applied to the idea of a deep state or shadowy cabal of unelected officials who truly hold power. This is a common theme in conspiracy theories, where the leader is presented as a figurehead, while the real power remains hidden behind a pseudonym of bureaucracy.

The use of anonymous sources can be seen as a form of pseudonymity in both journalism and political leaks. While sometimes it is necessary to protect individuals who are exposing wrongdoing, anonymous sources can also be used by leaders or their opponents to manipulate public opinion and spread unsubstantiated claims without taking responsibility.

4. The Interconnection

Those three concepts are interconnected. A leader's utopian rhetoric can be a tool to gain power, which is later used for greed (personal gain). The methods used to achieve this (propaganda or anonymous sources) can be seen as a form of pseudonym, designed to hide their true intentions.

The genuine desire for a better world, the corrupting influence of greed, and the use of deception to achieve either are defining features of modern political leadership. This is how I see these concepts apply to today's major world leaders.

Contemporary Leaders: Case Studies

1. Trump

(Greed) Accusations of greed have been central to Trump's public image and political career. His business background and frequent boasts about his wealth, as well as his perceived use of the presidency to benefit his personal businesses, are cited as examples of this. His focus on making a deal and winning at all costs can be interpreted as a form of greed for money, power, and dominance.

(Utopianism) Trump's rhetoric often taps into a form of populist utopianism. His campaign slogan, "Make America Great Again", suggests a nostalgic return to a perfect, idealized past. He presents a vision of a restored America, free from perceived threats and weaknesses, which functions as a nationalistic utopia for his supporters. This vision is in contrast with a pessimistic view of the present, framing his leadership as the only path to salvation.

(Pseudonym) Trump has famously used pseudonyms to speak to journalists and promote his business interests. This use of pseudonyms serves to create a false persona, allowing him to praise himself and his achievements anonymously. In a political context, this can be seen as a form of informational control and manipulation, where a leader can present a narrative without taking direct responsibility for it.

2. **Putin**

   (Greed) Putin's leadership is characterized as a kleptocracy, where a small, loyal elite, including himself, has enriched themselves through the control of state assets. The accumulation of immense personal wealth by Putin and his inner circle is a hallmark of his rule, demonstrating a powerful form of greed for money and absolute power.

   (Utopianism) Putin's political vision is a kind of reactionary utopianism. He presents a vision of a strong, unified Russia that has been restored to its former glory. This includes a rejection of Western liberal values and a return to traditional Russian national pride and morality. This is a utopia of the past, where Russia is a powerful and respected player on the world stage.

(Pseudonym) While Putin may not use pseudonyms in the same way as Trump, his government is widely accused of using pseudonyms in the form of anonymous online accounts, state-controlled media, and disinformation campaigns. These tools are used to spread pro-Kremlin narratives, attack opponents, and sow discord in other countries, while hiding the state's direct involvement.

3. **Musk**

(Greed) As the biggest billionaire on the globe, Musk's actions are viewed through the lens of greed. His relentless pursuit of market dominance for his various companies and his aggressive business tactics can be interpreted as a drive for wealth and influence. His focus on cost-cutting, and layoffs has drawn criticism and views of greedy prioritization of profit over employee well-being.

(Utopianism) Musk is arguably the most overtly utopian of this group. He frequently speaks of his companies' missions in grandiose terms. His rhetoric is a form of techno-utopianism where technology is the key to solving all humanity's problems and creating a better and more advanced future.

(Pseudonym) Musk does not use a fake name to speak to the press, but he has been accused of using anonymous or troll accounts on his own social media platform to promote his views and attacks. The platform "X" can be seen as a kind of digital pseudonym for his personal influence.

4. **Xi Jinping**

   (Greed) Xi's anti-corruption campaign is also seen, by many, as a tool to consolidate his personal power and eliminate political rivals. The accusations of greed are often directed at those he purges, but critics argue that the campaign serves a deeper, more profound greed for absolute control. The concentration of wealth and power within the communist party under his leadership is a key feature of his rule.

   (Utopianism) Xi's political ideology is a modern form of utopianism. He envisions a great modern socialist country and the great rejuvenation of the Chinese nation.

   (Pseudonym) The concept of pseudonym in China's political system is embodied in the state's use of vast propaganda. Information is heavily controlled. The voice of the state is a collective pseudonym that promotes Xi's vision while individual critics and dissenters are silenced or their identities are erased.

5. **Netanyahu**

   (Greed) His political career has been dogged by accusations of greed, particularly in the form of legal charges of fraud, breach of trust, and accepting bribes. These allegations suggest that his pursuit of power has been intertwined with personal and financial interests. The charges are a primary factor in the ongoing political instability.

(Utopianism) Netanyahu's rhetoric often centers on a nationalistic utopia of a secure and powerful Israel. He presents himself as the sole leader capable of protecting the nation from its enemies and ensuring its survival. This vision of a strong, dominant Israel is a form of political utopianism. That resonates with a significant portion of the electorate.

(Pseudonym) Netanyahu has been accused of using various political and media tools to obscure his true intentions and actions. His political messaging is carefully crafted to present a particular narrative, while his legal battles and the political machinations surrounding them can be seen as a way of using the pseudonym of the state's legal and political system to fight for personal survival and political dominance.

Regional Leaders

While some of the world's lesser leaders may not command the world stage in the same way as the US, China, and Russian presidents, their actions are often driven by the same fundamental forces on a more regional or national scale. Here are some of the lesser leaders who sometimes have a voice internationally, affected by the same concepts:

1. **Victor Orban (Hungary)**:

His allies, family members, and friends, through corrupt processes, have become extraordinarily wealthy.

He paints a picture of a sovereign, culturally homogeneous Hungary, protected from threats of Western liberal values, mass migration, and the European Union.

His government and political party use a vast and well-funded propaganda machine to spread their messages.

2. **Recep Tayyip Erdogan (Turkey):**

There are frequent accusations of corruption and the use of state resources to enrich his allies and family. He uses the state power to silence critics and seize their assets, manifesting a pattern of greed for political dominance and financial gain.

He presents himself as the leader who will restore Turkey's greatness and independence as a new and modern, powerful nation, returning to its Ottoman roots.

His government has been accused of using anonymous social media accounts to spread misinformation and manipulate public opinion.

3. **Robert Fico (Slovakia):**

His return to power and his efforts to dismantle anti-corruption institutions and reduce penalties for graft are seen as a clear manifestation of greed.

He presents a vision of a sovereign Slovakia, free from liberal tyranny and threats of illegal migration and foreign interference.

He often uses the pseudonym of state power to change laws and institutions to serve his personal and political interests.

4. Nicolas Maduro (Venezuela):

His greed for power brought him to repeatedly use the military, the judiciary, and other state institutions to suppress dissent and maintain his rule, even while his country was crumbling.

Maduro, to justify his policies and frame the opposition, uses the rhetoric of the socialist utopian vision he inherited from his predecessor, Hugo Chavez.

The manipulation of election results, the state-controlled media to present a false reality, and the creation of armed gangs to suppress opponents are pseudonyms to hide his methods.

5. Narendra Modi (India):

While not accused of personal financial greed, his policies are often seen as benefiting a small class of close business allies, which some critics argue is a form of crony capitalism, fueled by political greed for power.

Modi's vision is that of Hindu nationalism, presenting a picture of a strong, prosperous India that has reclaimed its historical and cultural glory, including the revocation of Kashmir's special status.

The networks used to promote Modi's agenda and attack his critics can spread disinformation, creating a pro-government narrative with aggression and anonymity.

Categorizing the Concepts

These concepts of greed, utopianism, and pseudonym can be categorized in multiple ways simultaneously, and that is the reason why they can be applied to all:

1. **Greed**

    - Financial greed
    - Political greed
    - Social greed
    - Experiential greed
    - Intellectual greed

2. **Utopianism**

    - Ecological utopias
    - Economic utopias
    - Political utopias
    - Technological utopias

3. **Pseudonym**

    - Pseudo-democrat
    - Pseudo-revolutionary
    - Pseudo-humanitarian
    - Pseudo-statesman

Miserere

- Pseudo-populist

Miserere and Misericordia to the illusions sold as hope.

And so let there be mercy and grace for all who seek it.

Mercy to the deserving, and even more to those who are not.

Chapter 10
Conspiracy Theories

Often one encounters, while socializing over a drink or a cup of coffee, some individuals who manifest negativity and contradictory symptoms that indicate beliefs in conspiracy theories, and evidently demonstrate infinite respect for those who write and promote conspiracy theories and also try to persuade others to read and absorb these theories regardless.

Defining Conspiracy Theories

Conspiracy theories are explanations of situations that invoke hidden, malevolent forces operating behind the scenes, rather than accepting the official narratives.

These theories propose that powerful entities control or manipulate outcomes, suppress the truth deliberately by ignoring or discrediting mainstream evidence.

Some characteristics of these theories are: the claims that the true story is hidden or censored, the belief that insiders know the truth and outsiders do not, and contradictory evidence is reinterpreted as part of the conspiracy.

Impact on Public Opinion

Conspiracy theories have had, throughout the years, a profound and troubling impact on public opinion, influencing everything from political beliefs to trust in science and institutions. Some theories have shaped the way people think and act:

Election fraud claims that led many to distrust democratic processes and public officials.

Conspiracies around climate change or vaccines have undermined public confidence, affecting health outcomes and environmental policies.

Radicalizing beliefs that push individuals towards extreme political movements or populist ideologies.

Shaping anti-immigration sentiment that leads to suspicion of "non-governmental organizations" (NGOs) in places like Libya and Tunisia.

False claims about wild fires and hurricanes being geo-engineered have disrupted emergency responses and spread distrust.

Spreading theories faster than factual information by promoting sensational content.

Misleading information content from social media platforms like "X" and "YouTube".

Individuals driven by conspiracy thinking have a tendency to view government performance negatively, especially when they feel their concerns are not being addressed.

Susceptibility of young generations to conspiracy narratives that offer alternative explanations for complex issues.

Influence on Elections

Conspiracy theories have played a significant role in shaping public perception and influencing electoral outcomes:

1. **United States**

    Claims of widespread voter fraud were pushed by Donald Trump in the 2020 presidential election.

    In the 2016 election, Russian interference suggested that foreign actors had manipulated public opinion via social media and hacked political organizations, fueling partisan divides and conspiracy theories.

2. **Japan**

    In 2025 (upper house elections), the right-wing Senseito party gained traction by promoting conspiracy theories about COVID-19, global elites, and immigration.

    Their rhetoric resonated with voters frustrated by inflation and foreign influence.

3. **Turkey**

    In the 2023 general election, President Erdogan's campaign circulated a doctored video falsely showing Kurdish militants endorsing the opposition, creating trauma and fears of national dismemberment among undecided voters.

In some cases, conspiracy theories have been used to shift attention during election cycles, such as repeated exposure to vague or sensational claims, which creates doubts amongst the electorate and shifts attention.

Common Conspiracy Theories

Some conspiracy theories are widespread enough to shape national conversations or policy, such as:

1. **Moon landing hoax** – Claiming the 1969 lunar landing was staged by NASA.

2. **9/11 inside job** – Accusations that the terror attacks were orchestrated by the U.S. government.

3. **Area 51 & aliens** – Beliefs that the U.S. government is hiding extraterrestrial life.

4. **Microchip vaccines** – Claims that COVID-19 vaccines contain tracking chips linked to Bill Gates.

5. **Pandemic as a hoax** – Beliefs that the virus was fabricated to control populations and boost pharmaceutical profits.

6. **Deep state** – The idea that a hidden network of government officials secretly controls policy, popularized during the Trump era.

7. **Princess Diana's death** – Some believe she was assassinated by British intelligence at the request of the royal family.

8. **Eat bugs** – A newer theory claiming elites are pushing insect-based diets to control the masses.

9. **Natural cures** – Claims that health authorities are hiding simple cures for diseases to protect the profits of big pharma companies.

10. **Chemtrails** – The erroneous beliefs that long-lasting condensation trails left in the sky by high-flying aircraft are chemtrails consisting of chemical agents sprayed for nefarious purposes.

Motivations for Promoting Conspiracy Theories

There are numerous factors that can drive an individual to actively create and spread conspiracy theories and narratives. These factors are social, cognitive, psychological, emotional, cultural, monetary gain, political gain, and entertainment. The big question is which one is plausible and credible, and which is fake?

World Leaders and Conspiracy Theories

Some key figures that can be associated with promoting conspiracy theories are:

Miserere

1. **Donald Trump (United States):**

He frequently promoted various conspiracy theories, including those related to the 2020 election ("stolen election" claims), the birth certificate of Barack Obama ("birtherism"), and various allegations against political opponents. More recently, he has commented on the Jeffrey Epstein death, with some of his supporters promoting conspiracy theories about it.

2. **Pierre Poilievre (Canada):**

The leader of the Conservative Party of Canada has been criticized for using rhetoric that echoes or flirts with conspiracy theories, particularly concerning the world economic forum (WEF) and claims of its alleged attempts to impose an agenda on sovereign governments.

3. **Jair Bolsonaro (Brazil):**

During his presidency, Bolsonaro was known for promoting various unsubstantiated claims and conspiracy theories, including mischaracterizing Nazism, and his former foreign minister also promoted theories about climate change.

4. **Nicolas Maduro (Venezuela):**

Maduro has been accused of promoting anti-Semitic conspiracy theories and claims of "Zionist" plots.

5. **Recep Tayyip Erdogan (Turkey):**

President Erdogan has a long history of employing conspiracy theories, particularly those related to a "mastermind" or foreign powers attempting to destabilize Turkey. He frequently blames external forces and shadowy international plots for domestic unrest, economic difficulties, or political opposition. While sometimes acknowledging the existence of a "deep state" in Turkey, his government has also used the concept to target perceived enemies within state institutions. A pervasive belief in Turkey is that foreign powers are constantly conspiring to weaken or dismember the Turkish Republic, often linked to the historical Treaty of Sèvres.

6. **Kais Saied (Tunisia):**

More recently, President Kais Saied has been noted for promoting conspiracy theories, particularly the "Great Replacement" theory. He claimed there was a conspiracy to change Tunisia's identity through mass migration, which subsequently fueled violence and hate against black people in the country.

7. **Vladimir Putin (Russia):**

The Russian state, under Putin's leadership, actively uses and promotes conspiracy theories as a tool of information warfare, both domestically and internationally. Narratives often portray Western nations (the US, NATO, EU) as conspiring to undermine Russia's sovereignty, expand their influence, and even target Russia directly. In Ukraine, during the invasion, Russia pushed the baseless conspiracy theory that the U.S. was funding secret bioweapons labs in Ukraine. While perhaps more of a personal conspiracy theory about Putin himself, the Kremlin has had to address rumors about him using body doubles, sometimes dismissing them while at other times fueling speculation.

Why Leaders Promote Conspiracy Theories

World leaders might promote such theories for a variety of reasons, including:

- **Mobilizing their base:** Conspiracy theories can energize and unite a specific segment of the population.
- **Distracting from problems:** Blaming external or secret forces can deflect attention from domestic issues or policy failures.
- **Discrediting opponents:** Framing political adversaries as part of a larger conspiracy can undermine their legitimacy.
- **Consolidating power:** By fostering distrust in established institutions, leaders can position themselves as the sole source of truth.

The spread of conspiracy theories by world leaders is a significant concern because it erodes trust in democratic institutions, hinders effective governance, and can lead to real-world consequences, including political violence and public health crises.

Psychological Motivations

The main motivation that induces individuals to write about and promote conspiracy theories is frustration, which can derive from a sense of injustice, lack of control, and powerlessness:

- **Existential Motives:** People have a fundamental need to feel safe, secure, and in control of their environment. When individuals experience events that cause significant anxiety, uncertainty, or a feeling of loss of control (like a pandemic, economic downturn, or major societal upheaval), they may seek explanations that provide a sense of order, even if those explanations are conspiratorial. Frustration with unexplained or chaotic events can lead to a desire for a clear, albeit fabricated, narrative.

- **Epistemic Motives:** There's a human need to understand the world, to have accuracy and subjective certainty. When official explanations for complex or disturbing events seem inadequate or unsatisfying, people may become frustrated and seek alternative explanations. Conspiracy theories often offer seemingly simple solutions to complex problems, which can be appealing to those struggling to make sense of things.

- **Social Motives:** People also have a need to maintain a positive self-image and feel good about the groups they belong to. If individuals or their group are marginalized, wronged, or unjustly treated, conspiracy theories can provide a framework that attributes blame to powerful "out-groups" and validates their feelings of victimhood or resentment. This can bolster self-esteem and group identity.

- **Resentment and Perceived Injustice:** Some research explicitly links feelings of resentment and perceived injustice to the development of conspiratorial worldviews. When individuals feel deeply wronged by society or powerful entities, conspiracy theories can become a way to process and express that anger and frustration, offering a narrative where those in power are malevolent and deserving of blame.

Impact on Governance

World leaders can be significantly affected by conspiracy theories in the political landscape in several ways:

- **Undermining institutions:** Conspiracy theories often posit that established institutions (governments, media, scientific bodies, international organizations) are secretly controlled by malevolent forces. This can severely erode public trust in these institutions, making it harder for leaders to govern effectively, implement policies and maintain social cohesion.

- Questioning leadership: When a significant portion of the population believes in conspiracy theories, they may view their leaders not as legitimate representatives, but as part of the "conspiracy" or as puppets of unseen powers. This can lead to decreased public cooperation, increased civil disobedience, and even challenges to democratic processes.

Political Polarization and Division:

- **Fueling extremism:** Conspiracy theories often thrive on "us vs. them" narratives, identifying clear enemies (e.g., "the deep state", "global elites"). This can exacerbate existing political divisions, push people towards more extreme ideologies, and make compromise and consensus-building more difficult.

- **Inciting Violence:** In extreme cases, belief in conspiracy theories has been linked to political violence. If people genuinely believe that powerful groups are engaged in sinister plots that threaten their way of life, they may feel justified in resorting to violence to "fight back".

Policy Challenges:

- **Public health crisis:** Conspiracy theories about vaccines, disease origins, or public health measures can directly hinder efforts to address national and global health crises, as seen during the COVID-19 pandemic.

Leaders face significant challenges in implementing effective public health strategies when large segments of the population distrust official information.

- **Climate change denial:** Conspiracy theories are prevalent in climate change denial, making it harder for leaders to garner public support for environmental policies and international climate agreements.

- **Foreign policy and international relations:** Conspiracy theories can impact a country's foreign policy by fostering distrust of other nations or international bodies. Leaders might face public pressure to act on the basis of unsubstantiated claims, or find it difficult to engage in diplomacy when their own population believes in plots involving foreign adversaries.

Manipulation and Disinformation:

- **Weaponization by adversaries:** State and non-state actors can intentionally create or amplify conspiracy theories as a form of political warfare and disinformation to destabilize adversaries, sow discord, and undermine democratic processes.

- **Exploitation by Populist Leaders:** Some political leaders, particularly populists, may strategically use or endorse conspiracy theories to mobilize their base, discredit opponents, and present themselves as the only ones willing to expose the "truth". This can be a powerful tool for gaining and maintaining power, even if it further erodes trust in established norms.

Impact on leaders themselves:

World leaders are often the direct targets of conspiracy theories, facing accusations of corruption, hidden agendas, or even malevolent intent. This can take a toll on their public image and personal well-being.

- **Decision-making:** While less common, a leader who genuinely believes in certain conspiracy theories might make policy decisions based on those unsubstantiated beliefs, leading to potentially disastrous outcomes.

The Appeal of Conspiracy Theories

When events seem random, unfair, or unexplainable, a conspiracy theory can provide a narrative that attributes negative outcomes to deliberate, hidden actions by powerful groups. Believing in secret plots, even malevolent ones, can ironically provide a sense of control.

Adhering to a conspiracy theory often means joining a community of like-minded individuals.

Conspiracy theories frequently offer straightforward but inaccurate explanations that bypass the need for understanding. Many individuals drawn to conspiracy theories feel a deep sense of frustration with everything around them.

Driven by contrarianism and a desire to challenge established narratives and conventional wisdom.

Once an individual begins to believe in a conspiracy, they are more likely to seek information to confirm their existing beliefs, while dismissing contradictory evidence.

Sometimes, some individuals may be more susceptible to conspiracy theories due to pre-existing psychological factors such as paranoia or narcissism.

The negative impact derived from conspiracy theories could be erosion of trust, real world harms, polarization and division, and distraction from real world issues.

A significant factor for most individuals who promote and those who believe in conspiracy theories is personal life frustrations.

During periods of uncertainty, stress, or perceived existential threats, people are more likely to seek explanations and turn to conspiracy theories to fill that void.

Superiority and Inferiority Complexes

In simple words, individuals who promote conspiracy theories are often suffering from a superiority complex, while those who believe in conspiracy theories suffer from inferiority complexes.

1. **Superiority Complex (or Inflated Sense of Self/Narcissism):**

- **Need for Uniqueness and Special Knowledge**: This is a strong driver. Believing in a conspiracy theory often means feeling privy to "hidden truths" that the "sheeple" or "mainstream" don't understand. This gives the believer a sense of intellectual superiority, special insight, and uniqueness. They are "awake while others are "asleep."

- **Grandiosity and Entitlement:** Some forms of narcissism involve grandiosity, a belief in one's own exceptionalism, and a sense of entitlement. Conspiracy theories can feed this by suggesting the believer is smarter, more perceptive, or morally superior for having "figured it out."

- **Contrarianism as Identity:** For those with a need to feel superior, being contrarian-automatically rejecting mainstream narratives-becomes a way to assert intellectual dominance. They don't just disagree; they believe they know better than everyone else.

- **Simplifying Complexities (Black and White Thinking)**: Narcissists often prefer clear-cut, black-and-white explanations. Conspiracy theories offer exactly that: a simple narrative of good versus evil, without the messy nuances and uncertainties of reality. This reinforces their sense of intellectual mastery over complex issues.

- **Projecting Malice:** If an individual views others (especially those in power) with suspicion or sees themselves as potential victims, they might project their own potential for manipulation or malevolence onto others. As some research suggests, "people who believe in conspiracy theories are often people who would be likely to conspire themselves."

2. **Inferiority Complex (or Underlying Feelings of Inadequacy, Insecurity):**

People who feel powerless or inadequate in their lives may be drawn to conspiracy theories because these theories offer a clear, albeit false, explanation for complex or distressing events. It can provide a sense that someone (even a "bad" someone) is in control, which can be less unsettling than chaos or random bad luck.

- **Externalizing Blame:** If someone feels a deep sense of personal failure or inadequacy, it can be psychologically comforting to attribute societal problems or personal misfortunes to an external, malevolent group (the conspirators). This shifts blame away from themselves or systemic issues that feel too overwhelming to address.

- **Validation of Suspicion:** For those with underlying insecurity or distrust, conspiracy theories validate their pre-existing suspicions about the world and powerful figures. It confirms their feeling that something is "off" or "not right," which can be a deeply held, albeit often unconscious, belief.

- **Need for Belonging:** Individuals feeling isolated or inadequate may find a sense of community and belonging within groups that share conspiratorial beliefs. This group validates their views and provides a social identity, counteracting feelings of loneliness or insignificance.

Distinguishing Credible from Fake

The characteristics of fake conspiracy theories can be attributed to:

- Lack of verifiable evidence
- Contradictory and unfeasible claims
- Overly simplistic explanations
- Sensational and emotional language
- Unreliable sources

The characteristics of credible claims can be attributed to:

- Logical and realistic scope
- Acknowledges complexity
- Open to falsification

Miserere and Misericordia to the truths buried beneath fear and fiction.

And so, let there be mercy and grace for all who seek it.

Miserere

Mercy to the deserving, and even more to those who are not.

John Ricciardi

Chapter 11
World 1968 Protests

The Golden Age and the Paradox of Prosperity

The decades 1946 to 1967, following World War II were economically prosperous for many western countries, and to a lesser extent, for the Eastern European bloc.

Western Europe, the United States, Japan and other capitalist economies experienced a remarkable period of sustained economic growth referred to as the "Golden Age of Capitalism." Countries enjoyed high GDP growth, full employment, rising living standards, industrial expansion, social progress and Marshall Plan aid (U.S. financial support). Eastern countries, under Soviet influence, also saw economic growth, experiencing industrial growth, limited consumer goods, and GDP growth.

In spite of this remarkable period, Europe experienced thousands of Europeans emigrate to North America and Australia, particularly from southern Italy.

The paradox of prosperity in Italy was so evident between northern elite and Southern poverty that migration became a way to escape poverty and to relieve demographic and economic pressure. Other European countries that experienced similar migration towards North America and Australia were:

- **Greece:** Escaping political instability, the Greeks settled mainly in Melbourne, Chicago, New York and Toronto.
- **Germany:** The economic collapse led many Germans to seek new lives abroad in Canada, U.S. and Australia.
- **Poland:** Many Poles escaped Soviet control to North America and Australia.
- **Hungary:** Many fled Soviet repression after 1956 Hungarian Revolution.
- **Netherlands:** Economic stagnation and housing shortages pushed many to migrate.
- **Britain:** Australia made migration extremely affordable through a scheme that promised a better life and good employment for just $10.
- **Spain:** Many escaped poverty and dictatorship (Franco).
- **Portugal:** Many escaped poverty and dictatorship (Salazar).

The Seeds of Unrest

For those who chose not to migrate but to stay behind in the hope of a better life, given the economic prosperity their countries were enjoying, a new generation was unwilling to accept the status quo, such as:

1. **Exposed Inequality:**

   - Economic growth highlighted who was left out (racial minorities, women, the working poor).
   - Expanded expansion of education, especially at the university level, gave students freedom to question authority, challenge norms and organize revolts.

2. **Media and Global Awareness:**

   - Television and radio brought civil rights abuses, war footage and global struggles into living rooms to the point where people could no longer ignore what was happening, so many became activists.

3. **Cultural Shift:**

   - Youth, in the 1960's, embraced counterculture, sexual liberation and anti-authoritarianism, and prosperity gave them the confidence to demand freedom, dignity and justice.

4. **Political Disillusionment:**

   - Governments were seen as slow to act on civil rights, complicit in war, and out of touch with the people, sparking outrage, such as the Vietnam War.

In other words, prosperity gave people the platform to protest. The 1960's protests shined a spotlight on deeply embedded systemic injustices across multiple areas of society such as:

1. **Education Inequality:**

    - Segregated schools with black students receiving inferior resources, outdated textbooks and overcrowded classrooms, facing exclusion and suppression.

2. **Housing Discrimination:**

    - Redlining policies denied black families access to mortgages and property values in blacks' neighborhoods were systematically undervalued.

3. **Criminal Justice and Policing:**

    - Black Americans were disproportionately targeted by police surveillance and brutality.
    - Peaceful protests were met with violent crackdowns such as the Selma march.

4. **Employment and Economic Inequality:**

    - Black workers faced job discrimination, lower wages and limited advancement opportunities.
    - Women earned significantly less than white men, fueling feminist protests.

5. **Health Care Disparities:**

- Black communities had limited access to quality health care and were mistreated by medical institutions.

6. Voting Rights Suppression:

- Southern states used poll taxes, literacy tests and intimidation to prevent black citizens from voting.

The Year of Revolution: 1968

These issues and more sparked the great students' protests of 1968 through the globe, culminating in social conflicts which were predominantly characterized by the rise of left-wing politics, anti-war sentiment, civil rights urgency, youth counterculture within the baby boomer generation and popular rebellions against military states and bureaucracies.

The protests of 1968 marked a turning point for the civil rights movement which produced revolutionary movements. The protests also sparked movements opposing the Vietnam War all over the United States, including in western European cities like London, Paris, Berlin and Rome, mostly dominated by students.

The most prominent manifestation was in France in May 1968, in which students linked up with wildcat strikes of up to ten million workers, giving the impression that the movement seemed capable of overthrowing the ruling government.

Miserere

In many other countries, struggles against dictatorship, political tension and authoritarian rule were also marked by protests in 1968. In the countries of Eastern Europe under communist parties, there were protests against the lack of freedom of speech and violations of other civil rights by the communist bureaucratic and military elites.

The protests of 1968 also expanded and escalated in Czechoslovakia, Poland, Yugoslavia, Japan and Egypt.

The protests that raged throughout 1968 included a large number of workers, students, and poor people facing increasingly violent state repression all around the world. Liberation from state repression itself was the most common current in all protests listed below. These refracted into a variety of social causes that reverberated with each other: in the United States alone, for example, protests for civil rights, against nuclear weapons and in opposition to the Vietnam War, and for women's liberation all came together during this year. Television, so influential in forming the political identity of this generation, became the tool of choice of the revolutionaries. They fought their battles not just in streets and college campuses, but also on television screens with media coverage. As the waves of protests of the 1960s intensified to a new high in 1968, repressive governments through widespread police crackdowns, shootings, executions, and even massacres marked social conflicts in Mexico, Brazil, Spain, Poland, Czechoslovakia, and China. In West Berlin, Rome, London, Paris, Italy, many Americans cities, and Argentina, labor unions and students played major roles and also suffered political repression.

The Eastern Bloc

The Eastern Bloc had already seen several mass protests in the decades following World War II, including the Hungarian Revolution, the uprising in East Germany and several labor strikes in Poland, especially important ones in Poznan in 1956. Waves of social movements throughout the 1960s began to shape the values of the generation who were students during 1968. In America, the civil rights movement was at its peak, but was also at its most violent, such as the assassination of Martin Luther King Jr. on April 4th by a white supremacist. In Northern Ireland, religious division paved the way for a decades-long violent conflict between Republicans and Irish Unionists. Italy and France were in the midst of a socialist movement. The New Left political movement was causing political upheavals in many European and South American countries. In China, the Cultural Revolution had reached its peak. The Arab-Israeli conflict had started in the early 20th century, the British anti-war movement had remained strong and African independence movements had continued to grow in number. In Poland in March 1968, student demonstrations at Warsaw University broke out when the government banned the performance of a play by Adam Mickiewicz (Dziady, written in 1824) at the Polish Theatre in Warsaw, on the grounds that it contained "anti-Soviet references". It became known as the March 1968 events.

Miserere

Social Movements Converge

The women's liberation movement caused generations of females to question the global status quo of unequal empowerment of women, and the post-war baby boomer generation came to reassess and redefine their priorities about marriage and motherhood. The peace movement made them question authority more than ever before. By the time they started college, the majority of young people identified with an anti-establishment culture, which became the impetus for the wave of rebellion and re-imagination that swept through campuses and throughout the world. College students of 1968 embraced progressive, liberal politics. Their progressive leanings and skepticism of authority were a significant impetus to the global protests in 1968.

Dramatic events in the year of the Soviet Bloc revealed that the radical leftist movement was ambivalent about its relationship with communism. The 2nd and 3rd June 1968, students' demonstrations in Yugoslavia, were the first mass protests in the country after the Second World War. The authorities suppressed the protests, while President Josip Broz Tito had the protests gradually cease by giving in to some of the students' demands. Protests also broke out in other capitals of the Yugoslavian Republics, Sarajevo, Zagreb, and Ljubljana, but they were smaller and shorter than in Belgrade.

In 1968, Czechoslovakia underwent a process known as the Prague Spring. In August 1968, during the Warsaw Pact invasion of Czechoslovakia, citizens responded to the attack on their sovereignty with passive resistance. Soviet troops were frustrated as street signs were painted over, their water supplies mysteriously shut off, and buildings decorated with flowers, flags, and slogans like, "An elephant cannot swallow a hedgehog."

Passers-by painted swastikas on the sides of Soviet tanks. Road signs in the country-side were over-painted to read, in Russian script, "Mockpa" (Moscow), as hints for the Soviet troops to leave the country. On 25th August 1968, eight Russian citizens staged a demonstration on Moscow's Red Square to protest the Soviet invasion of Czechoslovakia. After about five minutes, the demonstrators were beaten up and transferred to a police station. Seven of them received harsh sentences up to several years in prison.

Environmental and Civil Rights Movements

The environmental movement can trace its beginnings back to the protests of 1968. The environmental movement evolved from the anti-nuclear movement. France was particularly involved in environmental concerns. In 1968 the French Federation of Nature Protection Societies and the French branch of Friends of the Earth were formed and the French scientific community organized Survivre et Vivre (Survive and Live). The Club of Rome was formed in 1968. The Nordic countries were at the forefront of environmentalism. In Sweden, students protested against hydroelectric plans. In Denmark and the Netherlands, environmental action groups protested about pollution and other environmental issues. The Northern Ireland civil rights movement began to start, but resulted in the conflict now known as The Troubles. In January, police used clubs on 400 anti-war/anti-Vietnam protesters outside of a dinner for U.S. Secretary of State Rusk. In February, students from Harvard, Radcliffe, and Boston University held a four-day hunger strike to protest the Vietnam War. Ten thousand West Berlin students held a sit-in against American involvement in Vietnam. People in Canada protested the Vietnam War by mailing 5,000 copies of the paperback, Manual for Draft Age Immigrants to Canada to the United States. On March 6th, five hundred New York University (NYU) students demonstrated against Dow Chemical because the company was the principal manufacturer of napalm, used by the U.S. military in Vietnam. On March 17th, an anti-war demonstration in Grosvenor Square, London, ended with 86 people injured and 200 demonstrators arrested. Japanese students protested the presence of the American military in Japan because of the Vietnam War. In March, British students opposing the Vietnam War, physically attacked the British Defense Secretary, the Secretary of State for Education and the Home Secretary. In August, the 1968 Democratic National Convention in Chicago was disrupted by five days of street demonstrations by thousands of protesters. Chicago's mayor, Richard J. Daley, escalated the riots with excessive police presence and by ordering up the National Guard and the army to suppress the protests. On September 7th, the women's liberation movement gained international recognition when it demonstrated at the annual Miss America beauty pageant. The protest and its disruption of the pageant gave the issue of equal rights for women significant attention, and signaled the beginning of the end of beauty pageants, as any sort of aspiration for young females, and square-themed content in general.

1968 Protests Around the World

Here is where the protests of 1968 propagated and how:

1. **Brazil**: On March 28th, the Military Police of Brazil killed high school student Edson Luis de Lima Souto at a protest for cheaper meals at a restaurant for low-income students. The aftermath of his death generated one of the first major protests against the military dictatorship in Brazil and incited a national wave of anti-dictatorship student demonstrations throughout the year.

2. **Czechoslovakia and the Soviet Union:** In what became known as Prague Spring, Czechoslovakia's first secretary Alexander Dubcek began a period of reform, which gave way to outright civil protest, only ending when the USSR invaded the country in August. On August 25th, anti-war protesters gathered in Red Square only to be dispersed. It was titled the 1968 Red Square demonstration.

3. **France**: The French May 68 protests started with student protests over university reform and escalated into a month-long protest. The trade unions joined the protest, resulting in a general strike.

4. **Italy**: On March 1st, a clash known as the Battle of Valle Giulia took place between students and police in the faculty of architecture in the La Sapienza University of Rome. In March, Italian students closed the university for 12 days during an anti-war protest.

5. **Japan**: Protests in Japan, organized by the socialist student group Zengakuren, were held against the Vietnam War starting 17th January, with the visit of the USS Enterprise to Sasebo. In May, violent student protests erupted at multiple Japanese universities, having started earlier in the year from disputes between faculty and students for more student rights and lower tuition fees. Students occupied and clashed with staff, holding "trials" in public.

6. **Mexico**: Mexican university students mobilized to protest Mexican government authoritarianism and sought broad political and cultural changes in Mexico. The entire summer leading up to the opening of the 1968 Summer Olympics had a series of escalating conflicts between Mexican students with a broad base of non-student supporters and the police. Mexican President Gustavo Diaz

Ordaz saw the massive and largely peaceful demonstrations as a threat to Mexico's image on the world stage and to his government's ability to maintain order. On October 2nd, after a summer of protests against the Mexican government and the occupation of the central campus of the National Autonomous University (UNAM) by the army, a student demonstration in Tlatelolco Plaza in Mexico City ended with police, paratroopers and paramilitary units firing on students, killing and wounding an undetermined number of people. The suppression of the Mexican mobilization ended with the October 2nd massacre and the Olympic Games opened without further demonstrations, but the Olympics themselves were a focus of other political issues. The admittance of the South African team brought the issue of Apartheid to the 1968 Summer Olympics. After more than 40 teams threatened to boycott, the committee reconsidered and again banned the South African team. The Olympics were targeted as a high-profile venue to bring the Black Movement into public view. At a televised medal ceremony, black U.S. track stars John Carlos and Tommie Smith each raised one black-gloved hand in the Black Power salute, and the U.S. Olympic Committee sent them home immediately, albeit only after the International Olympic Committee threatened to send the entire track team home if the USOC did not.

7. **Pakistan**: In November 1968, the mass student movement erupted in Pakistan against the military dictatorship of Ayub Khan. The movement was later joined by workers, lawyers, white-collar employees, prostitutes and other social layers. Unprecedented class solidarity was displayed and the prejudices of religion, sex, ethnicity, race, nationality, clan or tribe evaporated in the red heat of revolutionary struggle. In 1968, at the height of the movement against him, young protesters in Karachi and Lahore began describing Ayub Khan as a dog ("Ayub Khan Kutta!"). Troops opened fire, killing dozens and injuring hundreds of students and workers. In March 1969, Ayub Khan resigned and handed power to Army Chief Yahiya Khan.

8. **Poland**: On January 30th, 300 student protesters from the University of Warsaw and the National Theater School were beaten with clubs by state-arranged anti-protestors. On March 8th, the 1968 Polish political crisis began with students from the University of Warsaw who marched for student rights and were beaten with clubs. The next day over two thousand students marched in protest of the police involvement on campus and were clubbed and arrested again. By March 11th, the general public had joined the protest in violent confrontations with students and police in the streets. The government fought a propaganda campaign against the protestors, labeling them Zionists. The 20 days of protest ended

when the state closed all of the universities and arrested more than a thousand students. Most Polish Jews left the country to avoid persecution by the government.

9. **South Africa**: In South Africa, the (white-only) University of Cape Town (UCT) Council's decision to rescind Archie Mafeje's (black) offer for a senior lecturer position due to pressure from the apartheid government angered students and led to protests on August 15th 1968 followed by a nine-day sit-in at the UCT administration building. Protesters faced intimidation from the government, anti-protestors, and fellow Afrikaans students from other universities. The police swiftly squashed support for the sit-in. In the aftermath, Mafeje left the country and did not return until 2000.

10. **Spain**: Compared to other countries, the repercussions of 1968 were much smaller in Spain, mostly being protests and strikes repressed by Franco's regime. Workers were joined by students at the University of Madrid to protest the involvement of police in demonstrations against dictator Francisco Franco's regime, demanding democracy, trade unions and worker rights, and education reform. In April, Spanish students protested against the actions of the Franco regime sanctioning a mass for Adolf Hitler. At the beginning of spring, the University of Madrid was closed for thirty-eight days due to student demonstrations.

11. **Sweden**: On May 3rd, activists protested the participation of two apartheid nations, Rhodesia and South Africa, in the international tennis competition held in Båstad, Sweden. The protest was among the most violent between Swedish police and demonstrators during the 1960s, resulting in a dialogue between the Swedish Government and organizers to curb the escalation of violence. The match was later played in secrecy, with Sweden winning 4-1. At Stockholm University, leftist students occupied their Student Union Building at Holländargatan from May 24th to 27th to send a political message to the government. Inspired by the protests in France earlier that month, the Stockholm protests were calmer than those in Paris. In reaction to the protests, right-wing students organized Borgerliga Studenter, or "Bourgeois Students", whose leaders included future prime ministers Carl Bildt and Fredrik Reinfeldt. The Student Union building would later be absorbed by the Stockholm School of Economics.

12. **Tunisia**: In Tunisia, a wave of student-led demonstrations and street protests in front of campuses began in March, inspired by protests in Poland and the 1968 protests in Egypt. Student protests, however, were quelled by police and the movement was crushed; in the short-lived period there were peaceful protests and demonstrations for one week.

13. **United Kingdom**: A series of art school occupations quickly spread throughout the UK during May and July 1968. The occupation at Hornsey College of Art (now Middlesex University) remains an emblematic event in the modern history of British universities. Cambridge students were involved in the Garden House riot on February 12th 1970.

14. **Northern Ireland:** On August 24th 1968, the Northern Ireland civil rights movement held its first civil rights march, from Coalisland to Dungannon. Many more marches were held over the following year. Loyalists (especially members of the UPV) attacked some of the marches and held counter-demonstrations in a bid to get the marches banned. Because of the lack of police reaction to the attacks, nationalists saw the RUC, almost wholly Protestant, as backing the loyalists and allowing the attacks to occur. On October 5th 1968, a civil rights march in Derry was banned by the Northern Ireland government. When marchers defied the ban, RUC officers surrounded the marchers and beat them indiscriminately and without provocation. More than 100 people were injured, including a number of nationalist politicians. The incident was filmed by television news crews and shown around the world. It caused outrage among Catholics and nationalists, sparking two days of rioting in Derry between nationalists and the RUC. A few days later, a student civil rights group—People's Democracy—

was formed in Belfast. In late November, O'Neill promised the civil rights movement some concessions, but these were seen as too little by nationalists and too much by loyalists.

15. **United States:** In the United States, the Civil Rights Movement had turned away from the South and toward the cities in the North and West with the issues of open housing and the Black Consciousness Movement. The civil rights movement unified and gained international recognition with the emergence of the Black Power and Black Panthers organizations. The Orangeburg Massacre on February 8th 1968, a civil rights protest in Orangeburg, South Carolina, turned deadly with the death of three college students. In March, students in North Carolina organized a sit-in at a local lunch counter that spread to 15 cities. In March, students from all five public high schools in East L.A. walked out of their classes protesting against unequal conditions in Los Angeles Unified School District high schools. Over the next several days, they inspired similar walkouts at fifteen other schools. On April 4th, the assassination of Martin Luther King Jr. sparked violent protests in more than 100 American cities, notably Louisville, Baltimore and Washington, D.C. On April 23rd, students at Columbia University protested and alleged the university had racist policies; three school officials were taken hostage for 24 hours. This was just one of a number of Columbia University

protests of 1968. The August 1968 Democratic National Convention became the venue for huge demonstrations against the Vietnam War and the Johnson Administration. It culminated in a riot, seen as part of television coverage of the convention, when Chicago police waded into crowds.

16. **West Germany:** The West German student movements were largely a reaction against the perceived authoritarianism and hypocrisy of the West German government and other Western governments. Particularly in relation to the poor living conditions of students. Students in 108 German universities protested to get recognition of East Germany, the removal of government officials with Nazi pasts and for the rights of students. In February, protests by professors at the German University of Bonn demanded the resignation of the university's president because of his involvement in the building of concentration camps during the war.

17. **Yugoslavia**: Protests in Yugoslavia, primarily centered at the University of Belgrade, had a significant impact on the political landscape under the leadership of Josip Broz Tito.

In 1968, Yugoslavia was under a unique communist self-management system, with Tito as its leader since the end of World War II. Despite enjoying relative independence from Soviet control, there were tensions within the country related to economic challenges, growing inequality, and authoritarianism. Students, in particular, felt frustrated by the gap between the promises of socialism and the reality of social and economic hardships.

The assassination of Che Guevara in October 1967, just prior to the student revolt of 1968, had a profoundly galvanizing impact on the student revolts globally, as Che was recognized as a martyr and icon of rebellion. While the 1968 revolts were driven by a wide array of factors, Che's martyrdom provided a unified international symbol that maximized his influence on the 1968 movement worldwide.

The Lasting Impact

These protests have become defining features of modern politics, with significant impact on world leaders and political systems:

Impact on world leaders – Protests have forced governments to reverse or modify policies.

The Indian government was compelled to repeal controversial farm laws after months of sustained protests.

Protests in Nigeria have been shown to influence fiscal redistribution, particularly in regions politically aligned with the government.

Protests have played a crucial role in demanding accountability from political leaders and the establishment of new democratic processes. Protests led to regime changes in Tunisia and Egypt and more recently in Malawi, where they forced an election re-run, resulting in the defeat of the ruling party.

While not immediately leading to policy changes, these protests dramatically shifted political conversations such as movements like "Black Life Matters" and "Fridays for the Future", which put issues on the global agenda, forcing politicians to address them.

A negative, yet significant, impact was that the protests caused increased use of repression by many governments. Many leaders, particularly in authoritarian regimes, have responded to dissent with violence, mass arrests and the passing of laws to restrict freedom of assembly and expression.

These protests, indeed, created new political parties and movements, and significantly influenced subsequent elections. This is particularly true in institutionalized democracies where protests have become a way for citizens to express discontent by demanding reforms.

While protests do not achieve all their goals, they often result in partial successes like wages increases and the repeal of specific laws.

A sustained long-term effort is required for these movements to be successful, such as civil rights and women's suffrage, which involved years of organization, coalition to build, and sustained pressure. The greatest influence on today's protests is the role of technology, which allows for rapid organization and global dissemination of information, however it sometimes backfires as governments also use technology for surveillance and to suppress dissent.

Worldwide protests are a powerful force and can be a vehicle for democratic change and accountability, while highlighting the fragility of democracy and the willingness of some leaders to use repression to maintain power.

Protests Beyond 1968

Beyond the widespread student protests of 1968, the last 200 years have seen numerous others protests and movements that impacted societies worldwide such as in the 19th, 20th and 21st centuries:

19th Century:

1. **Chartism (UK, 1838-1857):** This was a working-class movement advocating for political reforms, including universal male suffrage, secret ballots, and equal electoral districts. While their petitions were rejected, the movement highlighted widespread discontent and laid the groundwork for future reforms.
2. **Revolutions of 1848 (Europe):** A series of political upheavals spread across Europe, fueled by discontent with monarchical rule, social inequality, and lack

of political representation. These included movements for liberalism, nationalism, and socialism in France, Germany, Italy, and the Austrian Empire, among others.

3. **Women's Suffrage Movement (Late 19th to Early 20th Century, Global):** A sustained and widespread movement advocating for women's right to vote. This involved numerous protests, marches, and acts of civil disobedience, particularly prominent in the UK and the United States.

4. **Labor Movements (Global, throughout the 19th and 20th centuries):** The rise of industrialization led to widespread protests and strikes by workers demanding better wages, working conditions, and rights to organize. Examples include the Haymarket Affair in Chicago (1886) and countless strikes across industrializing nations.

20th Century (pre-1968 and post-1968):

1. **Russian Revolutions (1905 and 1917):** Mass protests, strikes, and uprisings against the Tsarist regime, eventually leading to the overthrow of the monarchy and the establishment of the Soviet Union.

2. **The Salt March (India, 1930):** Led by Mahatma Gandhi, this act of nonviolent civil disobedience protested British salt taxes and was a crucial moment in the Indian independence movement, mobilizing millions.

3. **Civil Rights Movement (United States, 1950s-1960s):** A pivotal movement demanding equal rights and an end to racial segregation and discrimination for African Americans. This involved sit-ins, marches (like the March on Washington for Jobs and Freedom in 1963), boycotts, and widespread nonviolent resistance.

4. **Anti-Vietnam War Protests (Global, 1960s-1970s):** While overlapping with the 1968 student protests, the anti-Vietnam War movement was a massive, sustained, and global phenomenon, with millions protesting the war's conduct and legitimacy.

5. **Tiananmen Square Protests (China, 1989):** Student-led pro-democracy protests in Beijing that were brutally suppressed by the Chinese government.

6. **The Baltic Way (Baltic States, 1989):** A peaceful political demonstration where over two million people formed a human chain spanning 600 kilometers across Estonia, Latvia, and Lithuania, demanding independence from the Soviet Union.

7. **Anti-Apartheid Movement (Global, 1980s-1990s):** A worldwide movement against the system of racial segregation and discrimination in South Africa, involving sanctions, boycotts, and mass demonstrations that contributed to the dismantling of apartheid.

21st Century:

1. **Anti-Iraq War Protests (Global, 2003):** Millions worldwide protested the impending invasion of Iraq, marking one of the largest coordinated protest events in history.
2. **Arab Spring (Middle East and North Africa, 2010-2012):** A series of anti-government protests, uprisings, and armed rebellions that spread across the Arab world, leading to significant political changes in several countries.
3. **Occupy Wall Street (United States, 2011):** A protest movement against economic inequality and corporate influence on politics, popularizing the phrase "We are the 99%."
4. **Black Lives Matter Protests (Global, 2013-Present):** A global movement against systemic racism and police violence, sparked by the killing of Trayvon Martin and later intensified by the murder of George Floyd, leading to widespread demonstrations and calls for police reform.
5. **Women's March (Global, 2017):** A worldwide protest advocating for women's rights and other social justice issues, held the day after the inauguration of President Donald Trump.

6. **Climate Strikes (Global, 2018-Present):** Inspired by Greta Thunberg, these ongoing global protests advocate for urgent action to address climate change.
7. **Indian Farmers Protest (India, 2020-2021):** Tens of thousands of farmers protested against new agricultural laws, leading to significant government concessions after prolonged demonstrations.

Why Protests Persist

So, the bottom line is that protests and movements are a form of public expression and political action, and a permanent feature of human societies. They will never cease due to:

- Political and economic disparities in wealth, power and opportunities. Those who feel marginalized organize protests.
- Fundamental freedoms remain the focus of ongoing protests such as civil rights, gender equality and LGBTQ rights.
- The rise of new ideologies, the climate crisis, and advancements in technology.
- Protests are foundational mechanisms for change, allowing ordinary people's voices to be heard.

And as societies evolve, new grievances will arise and people will continue to gather in the streets, online and in other spaces to demand changes.

John Ricciardi

Miserere and Misericordia to the voices that rose in chorus and the ears that turned away.

And so, let there be mercy and grace for all who seek it.

Mercy to the deserving, and even more to those who are not.

Chapter 12
Influencers

Today's world leaders are still adopting ideologies, theories, and methods of notorious past philosophers, diplomats, revolutionaries, historians, political theorists and economists, while advocating for reforms and changes in various systems before every election, such as political, economic, industrial, social, health and labor.

Here are some notorious philosophers that have influenced and continue to influence world leaders, as they adopt theories of those past diplomats and ideologists.

Classical Philosophers

Plato: Ancient Greek philosopher who had a profound impact on political theory, proposing the concept of a society where the leader is not motivated by personal gain, but by wisdom and deep understanding of justice, and where the most intellectual and moral individuals be in charge.

A modern leader can promise to improve education and reduce corruption, framing this as a pursuit of the Platonic ideal of a just society.

Machiavelli: An Italian philosopher promoting civic virtue, citizen armies, and public debate, emphasizing the importance of military strength for a stable state.

The Machiavellianism term, widely used today, refers to political cunning, manipulation and pragmatism.

Some of Machiavelli's ideas, which are today widely used, not only by political leaders, and are part of his work "The Prince", published in 1532, are:

◊ **Power Over Morality:**

- Machiavelli argued that a ruler should not be bound by traditional moral values if those values threaten the stability of the state.
- A prince must learn how not to be good, and know when to break promises, manipulate, or use force if needed.

◊ **Virtue vs. Fortuna:**

- Virtue: Not virtue in the Christian sense, but a ruler's strength, cunning, decisiveness, and adaptability.
- Fortuna: Fortune or chance. Machiavelli believed it controlled half of human affairs but the other half could be shaped by virtue.

◊ **Fear vs. Love:**

- A famous argument: "It is much safer to be feared than loved, if one must choose." Why? Love is fickle, fear is more reliable, as long as it doesn't turn into hatred.

- ◊ **The Lion and the Fox:**

  - A successful ruler must be both strong like a lion and clever like a fox, capable of spotting traps and defeating enemies.

- ◊ **Appearances Matter:**

  - A ruler must appear moral, generous, religious, and just, even if he is not, because people judge more by what they see than by what is real.

Machiavelli in Modern Politics

Machiavelli's insights are still very much alive today, and here is how they relate to modern politics:

- ◊ **Realpolitik:**

  - His thinking is reflected in pragmatic, power-driven politics, where national interest comes before ideology. Think of Henry Kissinger, Bismarck, or Putin, all influenced by realpolitik, a modern form of Machiavellian strategy.

- ◊ **Political Image-Making:**

  - Politicians today, like Machiavelli advised, craft public images carefully, even if they privately behave differently.
  - Example: A leader may preach peace while authorizing military action behind the scenes.

◊ **Campaign Strategy:**

- Election tactics often include controlled messaging, manipulation of truth, and strategic fear, techniques Machiavelli would not only recognize, but perhaps admire.

Controversial Leaders:

- Some leaders (e.g., Donald Trump, Vladimir Putin, Recep Erdogan) have been called "Machiavellian", not necessarily because they read The Prince, but because they act in self-serving, ruthless, or strategically manipulative ways.

Applying Machiavelli to Modern Leaders

Here is how Machiavelli's ideas can be applied to Donald Trump, Vladimir Putin, Benjamin Netanyahu, Xi Jinping, Recep Tayyip Erdogan and Elon Musk:

◊ **Donald Trump:**

- **Amoral Realism & Power-First Strategy:** Trump is often compared to Machiavelli for placing national interest and power above moral considerations. He treats global affairs like a business deal, friendly or adversarial depending on who pays more.
- **Fear as Political Leverage:** Trump's use of threats, from "fire and fury" to accusations

against the media, echoes Machiavelli's principle that being feared (but not hated) is more reliable than being loved.
- **Strongman Unpredictability ("Madman Theory"):** His unpredictable moves toward China, NATO, and in Gaza negotiations reflect a Machiavellian tactic: keep opponents off-balance to gain advantage.
- **Limits & Misinterpretations:** Critics argue Trump lacks true Machiavellian finesse, he often courts cruelty without strategic depth, which Machiavelli warned could breed hatred and weaken a ruler's position.

◊ **Vladimir Putin:**

- **Machiavellian Archetype:** Scholars describe Putin as a "Machiavellian grandmaster of geopolitical skullduggery".
- **Fear-Based Control with a Veneer of Legitimacy:** Like Machiavelli's advice, Putin uses fear and occasional popularity to maintain tight control over Russia.
- **Religion as a Political Cloak:** He aligns closely with the Russian Orthodox Church to justify policy moves, a tactic Machiavelli praised for shrouding political aims in moral authority.

- **Hybrid Warfare & Virtue:** Putin's strategic mix of coercion, cyber tactics, intelligence operations, and conventional force embodies Machiavelli's concept of virtuosity in mastering fortune.

◊ **Benjamin Netanyahu:**

- **Authoritarian and Populist Governance:** Netanyahu's recent focus on judicial overhaul, media censorship, and aligning with illiberal allies suggests a power-centric, authoritarian approach, resonant with Machiavellian pragmatism.
- **"Poison Machine" Strategy:** He's been described as deploying Machiavellian tactics, targeted campaigns to weaken political opponents and erode democratic checks.
- **Media Manipulation & Judicial Reshaping:** Controlling narratives and reshaping institutions aligns with Machiavelli's stress on managing perception and consolidating power, even at the expense of democratic norms.

◊ **Xi Jinping, The Technocratic Machiavellian:**

- Total Control of State & Narrative: Xi centralized power like no leader since Mao: purged rivals, dismantled term limits, and now dominates the Party, military, and state. Like Machiavelli advised, he eliminated threats before they became dangerous.

- **Use of Fear and Force Without Open Violence:** Repression is discreet and institutional: censorship, surveillance (e.g., social credit system), and "re-education" in Xinjiang. It maintains fear without direct hatred, as Machiavelli suggested.
- **Appearance of Virtue:** Xi projects himself as a Confucian reformer, anti-corruption crusader, and savior of China's rise, maintaining the image of virtue while using strategic repression beneath the surface.
- **Fortuna and Virtue:** Xi used the 2008 financial crisis and Western democratic fatigue to reinforce China's stability narrative. He shaped China's destiny with confidence, like a true Machiavellian.

◊ **Recep Tayyip Erdogan, The Populist Sultan:**

- **Survivalist Adaptability:** Erdogan evolved from reformist mayor to Islamist populist to strongman president. His chameleon-like transformation reflects Machiavelli's advice to adapt as fortune changes.
- **Strategic Use of Religion:** He recentered Turkish identity around Islam and nationalism, including reconverting Hagia Sophia to a mosque. Machiavelli advised rulers to use religion to unify people.

- **Fear Through Institutional Control:** Post-2016 coup purges targeted journalists, academics, and judges. Erdogan used crisis to justify emergency powers and crush dissent, fear used surgically, not chaotically.
- **Appearances Over Substance:** Despite economic crises and repression, Erdogan presents himself as a man of the people, anti-elitist, protector of faith, all carefully maintained illusions.

◊ **Elon Musk, The Corporate Machiavellian:**

- **Master of Narrative and Image:** Musk curates a mythos: visionary innovator, rebel billionaire, meme lord. Like Machiavelli said, rulers must appear virtuous, even if their methods are not.
- **Use of Fear and Authority in Business:** He often fires large teams, issues ultimatums (e.g., "hardcore Twitter 2.0"), and leverages fear to maintain authority. He openly mocks norms, a move Machiavelli might admire.
- **Disregard for Morality When Needed:** Musk pushes ethical boundaries (AI safety, X censorship, labor disputes) if they interfere with expansion, reflecting the Machiavellian mindset that results justify the means.
- **Controlling Fortuna Through Virtue**: He turns crises into branding moments. SEC lawsuit,

Twitter chaos, or rocket failures become symbols of resilience, not weakness.

Modern Political Theorists

John Locke: An English philosopher of the 17th century, is considered one of the most influential thinkers who laid the foundation for modern liberalism.

His theories are foundational to most western democracies. Today the principals of limited government, individual rights and the consent of the governed are cornerstones of many constitutions and political systems.

Adam Smith: A Scottish economist and philosopher, widely regarded as the father of economics. He argued that an economy flourishes when individuals are free to pursue their own self-interest in a free market without government interference.

Many world leaders today, particularly in capitalist nations, base their policies on his principles of free trade, deregulation and low taxes, leading to greater national prosperity.

Karl Marx: A German philosopher, economist, historian, journalist and revolutionary socialist whose ideas form the base of Marxism. Came from a well-to-do family of Jewish heritage converted to Christianity. Due to his radical views, he was suppressed by the Prussian government and expelled from Germany. His continuous radical writing caused his expulsion from France and Belgium before finally settling in London as a stateless exile.

John Ricciardi

The Communist Manifesto he and his co-author Engels wrote in 1848 laid out the principles of communism. Central to his thought are the concepts of class struggle between the "bourgeoisie" (the owners) and the "proletariat" (the working class) and the idea that capitalism's inherent contradictions would inevitably lead to a proletarian revolution and the establishment of a classless communist society.

Marx's theories continue to have significant influence on today's world leaders. His concepts of class struggle, exploitation and alienation, provide a powerful vocabulary for leaders and political movements, to analyze and criticize the flaws of the capitalist system. Marx's theories help leaders identify problems like persistent unemployment, financial crises and the power imbalance between workers and employers.

While Marx's ideas directly fueled the rise of socialist and communist political parties worldwide, many modern leaders in democratic countries are influenced by a more moderate democratic socialist tradition, which advocates for a mixed economy that combines capitalist markets with social welfare programs, strong labor protections and wealth distribution.

Leaders in social-democratic nations draw on Marx's ideas to justify their policies, and to help them analyze the root causes of conflicts and social instability.

Selective Application of Philosophy

Today's world leaders use past philosophers' frameworks in a way that serves their political goals. My cynical interpretation is that:

When an economy is booming, a leader can praise the success by invoking the power of free markets. This frames their policies as a triumph of economic principals, giving them philosophical justification for their success.

When things go wrong, leaders use the same philosophies to deflect blame and explain away their failures, or shift the blame to external forces for not fully embracing the principles.

In a sense, these philosophers' philosophies are living, breathing political tools that leaders use to:

- Provide a coherent narrative
- Legitimize their power
- Mobilize followers

Leaders rarely apply these philosophies in a pure academic sense, and they selectively choose the parts that support their agenda, using the prestige and weight of these great thinkers to lend credibility to their own actions and rhetoric.

The Transition from Philosophy to Performance

The philosophers spoke in shadow and syllogism: they questioned justice, imagined ideal Republics, and dissected the anatomy of power long before it wore a crown.

Their influence was foundational, but today influence wears a different face.

We have moved from the academy to algorithm, from the contemplative to the curated, and from philosopher to performer.

The modern leader is no longer merely a statesman, but a persona.

They are influencers, shaping public sentiments not through reasoned discourse, but through optics, virality and emotional resonance.

Where the writer dissects injustice, the song writer amplifies it. Where the novelist builds a world, the musician shakes the one we live in. From the novels of resistance to the ballads of protests, the message remains. Songs are literature in motion; they carry the weight of history and the urgency of now. They do not wait to be studied, they demand to be felt.

And so we turn the page from the quiet of the written word, to the thunder of the sung truth. Chapter 13, Leaders as Influencers.

Miserere and Misericordia to the minds who questioned justice before it was politicized, who dissected power before it was performed and who imagined virtue not as branding, but as burden.

Miserere and Misericordia to the thinkers who warned us, to the leaders who forgot.

Miserere

And so, let there be mercy and grace for all who seek it.

Mercy to the deserving, and even more to those who are not.

Chapter 13
Leaders as Influencers

In this chapter, I want to talk about how world leaders (politicians, monarchs, religious, economic tech moguls and celebrities) can influence the general public in several ways, particularly by triggering "jealousy and envy".

Two Faces of Envy

There are two faces of envy, benign envy and malicious envy:

1. Benign envy is more like aspiration where people are motivated to emulate them.
2. Malicious envy is when people feel populist backlash against leaders who display extravagant lifestyles while the public struggles.

Visible wealth, privileges, charisma, popularity, access to power and symbolic victories are all behaviors that can and will trigger jealousy and envy. Leaders may shape public behaviors with admiration from supporters, culture imitation, populist revolt and para-social identification.

Historical and Modern Examples

Some examples, historically and in modern times, are:

- Julius Caesar, admired by the masses for his popularity, which led to his assassination.

- Cleopatra's beauty, influence and wealth stirred envy across courts and empires.
- Donald Trump's supporters admire his wealth and defiance of convention, while detractors see those same traits as undeserved and provocative.
- Elon Musk, seen as an innovator and visionary by some, envied for his fortune and influence by others.

Relatability, achievement, success and selective humility are all qualities that induce supporters to a benign envy status.

Flaunting privilege, winning publicly and mocking outsiders are flaws that spark malicious envy.

Personal Impact

Unfortunately, jealousy towards world leaders often spills into personal relationships (also because it is the easiest and justifiable way to discharge proper frustrations), creating conflicts with friends and family.

These are the easiest and best targets for individuals to discharge their stressful frustrations, mostly due to their own negligence, and they often hide behind denouncing world leaders to mask their own failures. They focus on the wealth gap, status anxiety, and perceived injustice.

- Political polarization at the dinner table may lead to arguments with relatives who admire or defend the significant leader.
- Seeing a glamorous or successful leader may make a person more sensitive to differences with people around them.
- Status competition within a family can occur when someone becomes resentful towards immediate family members for not providing the same lifestyle of the leaders he watches indulge.

Psychological Mechanisms

Then there is the psychological mechanism of:

- External envy (toward leaders)
- Internal insecurity (I am not good enough, life is unfair)
- Projection and comparisons with close people
- Conflict and resentment in personal relationships

The dynamics of these envy/jealousy manifestations can be expressed in the below examples:

- Trump/Biden families in the U.S. have cut off contact over disagreements often fueled by emotions tied to envy or resentment towards what each leader represents.
- Envy towards perceived pampered lifestyles of royals (the Royal family in the UK) can make some people

more sensitive about social class, leading to friction with wealthier friends or relatives.
- In the tech billionaires circle, envy towards Musk, Bezos, Zuckerberg etc., and their wealth can heighten feelings of rivalry toward peers in similar industries.

Admiration towards leaders tends to bond people with similar views but can create cliques within families and friends, while malicious envy often divides by amplifying insecurities, competitiveness and ideological rifts.

Emotional and Social Dynamics

1. **Emotional spillover:** People carry the pride, frustration and insecurity they feel into their everyday interactions. This can make them warmer and more inclusive towards like-minded relatives or colder and argumentative towards those who disagree.
2. **Identity-driven division:** Supporters may form tighter bonds with family and friends who share their admiration. Opponents may be viewed as personally threatening, even when disagreements are political in nature. This can fracture families and friendships.
3. **Status and comparison tension:** This fuels sibling rivalry, spousal dissatisfaction, or competitiveness among friends.
4. **Polarization as social norm:** At family gatherings, debates become proxy battles over the leader's image.

People may avoid certain relatives altogether to sidestep tension.

5. **Long-term impact:** Over time, these emotional patterns can erode trust and intimacy, replacing them with conditional relationships based on political alignment or shared resentment and admiration.

In a short sense, world leaders become stand-in parents or team captains, and people fall into childlike loyalty patterns complete with jealousy, in-group favoritism, and tantrums when they feel their side is losing. If we strip away politics, the behavior of people is not much different from kids.

Fighting over which superhero is cooler, except that now the superhero controls nuclear codes or the global economy.

One last point I want to make is that kids do not hold grudges as opposed to adults that can go a lifetime without talking to one another.

From Leadership to Art

Leadership today is often measured by visibility, not vision. The modern leader curates influence through optics, slogans and digital charisma, but beneath the surface of performance lies a quieter force, one that seeks understanding and not applause.

Literary artists have long stood in contrast to political spectacle. They do not govern nations, but they interrogate them. They do not draft laws, but expose their consequences. They do not command armies, but they mobilize minds.

Miserere

From Dostoevsky's moral labyrinths to Baldwin's searing truths, from Achebe's post-colonial reckoning to Atwood's dystopian warnings, the writer becomes a mirror, a scalpel, a lantern.

Where leaders shape perception, literary artists shape conscience.

Next chapter 14 (Literary Artists) will elaborate further on these artists of global literature and their influence.

Miserere and Misericordia to the rulers who speak in hashtags, and govern with applause instead of wisdom.

And so, let there be mercy and grace for all who seek it.

Mercy to the deserving, and even more to those who are not

Chapter 14
Literary Artists

A Coffee Shop Confrontation

Shortly after the Russian invasion of Ukraine, while sipping a nice cup of coffee with friends at a coffee shop, I was asked what was my view on Russia invading Ukraine. I responded by saying that it was insane to witness general civilians lose their lives for the caprices of some leaders, and when I suggested humorously to ship volumes of Leo Tolstoy's "War and Peace" to the Kremlin, so that Vladimir Putin and his immediate subordinates could revisit and reread the masterful piece of literature, to reflect on what was happening, I was aggressively reprimanded and bombarded with insults, some as far as saying that Putin was the most intelligent person on earth and that I had no right to suggest that. Needless to say that these individuals are not friends any longer, but they regret vividly having reacted to me in such a vigorous manner.

Literature as Mirror to War

Having briefly described my personal experience, I want now to elaborate on various literature that some world-renowned writers have written about conflicts, hoping that someday world leaders will reflect on that. Here are some authors whose work has helped create a more informed, critical and skeptical global public to the point that world leaders must think more carefully about the justification for war and the consequences of their actions.

Tolstoy: War as Senseless Chaos

- Leo Tolstoy's "War and Peace", while it chronicles the French invasion of Russia, is not a glorification of battle, but Tolstoy uses the scope of the novel to show war as a chaotic, senseless force driven by the vanity of a leader (Napoleon) whose caprices brought immense suffering to ordinary people.
- In "The Kingdom of God Is Within You", Tolstoy took a more pacifist stance arguing against violence in all forms, based on his Christian beliefs. In fact, his ideas on non-violent resistance, profoundly influenced figures like Mahatma Gandhi.

Hemingway: Stripping Away Glory

- Ernest Hemingway's "A Farewell to Arms", while based on his personal experience as an ambulance driver in WWI, is a direct critique of the notions of war. He strips away concepts of glory, honor and patriotism, presenting war as a brutal, meaningless affair that causes physical and psychological trauma.

Other Voices Against War

In addition to Tolstoy and Hemingway, many other authors have written powerful anti-war literature, exploring the psychological toll of conflict, the absurdity of violence and the disillusionment that follows:

- Erich Maria Remarque, a German veteran of war whose "All Quiet on the Western Front", details the mental anguish of a young German soldier.
- Henri Barbusse, a French soldier whose "Under Fire" novel offers a stark look at trench warfare and the daily suffering of the infantry.
- John Dos Passos, an American ambulance driver whose novel "Three Soldiers" focuses on three American servicemen and their disillusionment with the war.
- Siegfried Sassoon and Wilfred Owen: two English poets, who served in the front lines, created some of the most visceral and widely read anti-war poetry.
- Kurt Vonnegut: a prisoner of war, whose "Slaughterhouse-Five" novel talked about the absurdity of war.
- Joseph Heller: whose satirical novel "Catch-22" became a classic of antiwar literature, exposing the irrationality of military bureaucracy.
- Norman Mailer: a U.S. Army veteran who wrote "The Naked and the Dead", a novel about an American platoon fighting in the Pacific.
- Dalton Trumbo: whose novel "Johnny Got His Gun" tells the story of an American soldier who is severely disfigured.

- Tim O'Brien: a veteran of the Vietnam War, whose work "The Things They Carried" is celebrated for its exploration of memory, truth, and the burdens soldiers carry.
- Michael Herr: a war correspondent whose book "Dispatches" is a work of new journalism that captures the surreal, hallucinatory and chaotic experience of the war.
- Jaroslav Hašek: a Czech writer whose unfinished satirical novel "The Good Soldier Švejk" is a powerful critique of military authority and the senselessness of war.
- Stephen Crane: his novel "The Red Badge of Courage" is a work focusing on the psychological experience of a young soldier in battle.

Impact on Public Consciousness

These literary works have had a profound impact on public opinion, which in turn influences political leaders.

The phrases "Lost Generations" and "Catch-22" are part of our vocabulary. Leaders today operate within this cultural context where the glorification of war is often met with cynicism and skepticism.

Anti-war literature often focuses on the common humanity of soldiers on all sides of a conflict. Political leaders today are more likely to face a public that is, at least in some segments, resistant to simplistic narratives.

Even if leaders have not read specific books, anti-war literature contributes to this collective historical memory, making it harder for leaders to ignore the potential for disaster and the human cost of their decisions.

A real and possible influence some leaders may have from these literary works on a personal level, could be that as young persons, reading them may have shifted their worldview, and they may carry that perspective with them throughout their careers and lives. In essence, these authors don't serve as policy handbooks for world leaders, but their work has helped create a more informed, critical and skeptical global public.

Students and Tolstoy's Protest

Shortly after the invasion of Ukraine, students held protests in which they used one of the most revered works of Russian literature, to make their point. They were drawing a direct comparison between the invasion of Ukraine and Tolstoy's portrayal of Napoleon's invasion of Russia.

In an environment where simply saying the word "war" was banned, using a book as a symbol was a clever way to protest. Here the students demonstrated by flashing the book "War and Peace", a high form of diplomacy, intellectuality, and moral resistance against a regime that was trying to control actions and thoughts.

World leaders shall take note, behave and act accordingly rather than being overcome by their caprices, arrogance and impulsivity.

Miserere

From Page to Stage

The literary artist writes in solitude, crafting sentences that interrogate, illuminate and endure. Their words live on paper, in silence, waiting to be read and remembered. But some truths demand more than reflection, they demand resonance. And so the pen becomes a microphone, the metaphor becomes a melody, the critique becomes a chorus.

Where the writer dissects injustice, the song writer amplifies it. Where the novelist builds a world, the musician shakes the one we live in. From the novels of resistance to the ballads of protests, the message remains. Songs are literature in motion; they carry the weight of history and the urgency of now. They do not wait to be studied, they demand to be felt.

And so we turn the page from the quiet of the written word, to the thunder of the sung truth. Chapter 15, Entertainment Artists.

Miserere and Misericordia to the pens that bled truth and the pages that dared to disturb.

And so, let there be mercy and grace for those who seek it.

Mercy to the deserving, and even more to those who are not.

John Ricciardi

Chapter 15
Entertainment Artists

Songs We Hear But Don't Listen To

As I was inspired to write this book when I heard the song "Miserere" sung by Pavarotti and Zucchero, I was drawn to reflect deeply after hearing "Imagine", "One Love" and "What's Going On" and I said to myself why have people not heard and do not hear these songs; maybe they do not understand the true meaning.

While these songs are ubiquitous, continuously sung by many at various events, they are often heard, but not truly listened to:

- "Imagine", a feel-good anthem.
- "One Love" sells unity.
- "What's Going On" is mournful.

Why These Songs Haven't Changed the World

Other reasons these songs have not helped change the world (yet) are:

Symbolism Over Substance:

- World leaders may quote these songs, but rarely embody their principles.
- The general public, while feeling moved, don't mobilize.

- These songs become, symbols of peace without provoking the discomfort needed for change.

Misinterpretation:

- "Imagine no possessions" is not just poetic, it is anti-capitalism.
- "One Love" is not just romantic, it is a call for post-colonial unity.
- "What's Going On" is not just soulful, it's a protest against war, racism and neglect.

Resistance to Change:

- People may resonate emotionally but resist intellectually. Leaders often dismiss art as idealistic or naïve.
- The public may feel overwhelmed, cynical or powerless.

So, some people understand the true meaning, some do not, and even among those that do, few are willing to confront what those meanings demand of them. Here they are:

1. **Imagine (John Lennon)** "Imagine there's no countries"

2. **One Love (Bob Marley)** "Let's join together and a-feel alright"

3. **What's Going On (Marvin Gaye)** "Bring some lovin' here today"

John Ricciardi

The Paradox of Ubiquity

We live in a world where "Imagine," "One Love," and "What's Going On" echo through stadiums, commercials and commemorations. They are sung at vigils and played at protests. They are quoted by presidents and posted by influencers. And yet, despite their ubiquity, despite their beauty, despite their power, something remains unchanged.

These song melodies soothe but their messages unsettle if we dare listen, but most do not.

We hum along to "Imagine", forgetting that it asks us to dismantle religion, borders and wealth. We sway to "One Love", forgetting that it was born from the fire of colonial resistance and Rastafarian prophecy. We mourn with "What's Going On", forgetting that it indicts war, racism and political apathy.

World leaders invoke these songs as symbols of unity, but rarely as calls to actions. The general public embraces their emotional resonance, but not their intellectual demands. These songs are not just poetic, they are political. And politics, when inconvenient, is often silenced.

The Songs and Their Meanings

1. **Imagine (John Lennon)**: "Imagine" was composed by John Lennon in 1971 where he invited everybody to envision a world built on shared humanity, calling for the deconstruction of ideology and the em-

brace of global unity. "Imagine" has been used in moments of grief, protest and hope, becoming a universal anthem for peace.

2. **One Love (Bob Marley)** "One Love" was composed by Bob Marley in 1965, reworked in 1977. Marley's call here is to transcend race, religion, and politics. The song blends Rastafarian values with civil rights themes, offering redemption even for the hopeless sinner.

3. **What's Going On (Marvin Gaye)** "What's Going On" was composed by Marvin Gaye in 1971 to respond to social unrest and the Vietnam War. The song is both personal and political, where he challenges the authorities when he says that war is not the answer.

These songs continue to inspire movements from climate justice to antiracism, used in campaigns for racial equality, refugee rights, and global solidarity and blending soul with social consciousness. They are not just nostalgic, but living tools for resistance.

Other Voices of Protest

There are many more artists who composed protest and anti-war songs:

- Bob Dylan, "The Times They Are a-Changin'"
- Joan Baez, "Where Have All the Flowers Gone"
- Phil Ochs, "I Ain't Marchin' Anymore"

- Pete Seeger, "Waist Deep in the Big Muddy"
- Neil Young, "Ohio"
- Billy Bragg, "Between the Wars"
- Michael Franti, "Bomb the World"

From Songs to Dreams

A song ends, but its echo lingers, it stirs something deeper, beyond rhythm, beyond rhyme, it awakens the dreamer. The ones who hear not just the notes, but the call, who see not just as it is but as it could be, they hum the melody while sketching blueprints for change.

Dreamers are the inheritors of every verse that dared to hope, they take the raw emotion of music and mold it into vision, they are the architects of possibility, fueled by lyrics and longing.

Where songs ignite, dreamers build.

Where music moves, dreamers march, they are the ones who imagine the next stanza not in sound, but in steps.

So let the music fade, let the silence swell, and in that stillness, watch the dreamers rise.

Miserere and Misericordia to the verses that we sang but never understood, and the chords that carried warnings we refused to hear.

And so, let there be mercy and grace for all who seek it.

Mercy to the deserving, and even more to those who are not.

Chapter 16
Dreamers

Four Friends at the Bar

There is an Italian song "Quattro Amici al Bar" (Four Friends at the Bar), composed in 1991 by singer and song-writer Gino Paoli, which inspired me to close out the book with this chapter.

In some of the previous chapters, I often make reference to friends at the bar, socializing and conversing over a cup of coffee.

This song reflects on time, friendship, and the evolution of dreams and ideals. The song tells the story of four young friends who, over drinks at a bar, passionately discuss changing the world, making revolutions, and achieving great things. As time passes, they meet again and their youthful idealism has faded into the routine of adult life, and established society. This disillusionment is anti-status quo and anti-conformity, which can be seen as a critique of the systems that perpetuate conflict and social problems.

Nostalgia and Disillusionment

This song evokes a sense of nostalgia for a time of pure idealism, contrasting with the harsh realities of growing up and the compromises life demands. It questions whether change is possible or if individuals are inevitably absorbed by the very system they once sought to challenge.

By highlighting the transformation from passionate revolutionaries to professionals within the system, the song implicitly questions the efficacy of political and social movements, and the pressure to conform. This subtle critique of the establishment can be seen as a distant echo of antiwar sentiments, as war is often a product of established power structures.

It is less about a direct message against war, and more about the fading of youthful dreams for a better world, which would inherently be a world without war.

"Quattro Amici al Bar" is a masterpiece of Italian songwriting that delves into the human condition. While not an explicit anti-war anthem, its themes of hope, disillusionment, the passage of time and the enduring power of human connection subtly align with anti-war sentiments, by advocating for a world built on different values than conflict and destruction. It is a profound reflection on society and humanity, which, as such, serves as an indirect form of social and political commentary.

The Song

Quattro Amici al Bar (Gino Paoli):

Sono qui, con quattro amici al bar, che hanno voglia di cambiare il mondo.

Miserere

They wrote, they sang, they warned but the world did not listen.

And now, in the quiet of a bar, one sits alone, the others are gone, lost to comfort, compromise or silence.

Then four young voices rise again, they speak of liberty, of change and hope.

And so, the song begins anew.

Miserere, Misericordia, let them not be forgotten.

The Dreamers

They were writers, singers and poets. They were the ones who dared to speak when silence was safer.

Tolstoy wrote of conscience and war. Victor Jara sang until they broke his hands. Nina Simone turned rage into melody. Bob Dylan asked questions no one wanted to answer. They believed art could awaken the soul, words could change the world, and so did we.

We gathered in cafes and bars, in basements and bedrooms, with guitars and burning hearts, we spoke of liberty, of justice, of revolution, we were four friends at the bar.

The Fade

But time is a quiet thief, one by one the voices faded. One took a job, one fell in love, one got tired, one stayed behind, still talking to ghosts. The world did not change, the songs were sung, the books were written, but the world did not change.

The Echo

And then one day in the same bar, four teenagers walked in. They spoke of liberty, of justice, of revolution, they were laughing, they were dreaming, they were us. And nothing had changed and everything had begun again.

Benediction

Eravamo quattro amici al bar che volevano cambiare il mondo.

(We were four friends at the bar, that wanted to change the world)

Let this be the song at the end of the world, let it be heard, let it be remembered, let it be sung again.

From Words to Action

From the solitude of the writer's desk, to the roar of the protest, from songs to the quiet resolve of the dreamer, a single thread runs through it all, the courage to imagine. Literature gave us language, music gave us momentum, dreamers gave us direction.

Each word written, each note sung, each vision held, is a defiance of silence, of apathy, of despair. Together, they form a tapestry of resistance and renewal.

So, whether you write, sing, or dream, you are part of the future.

Let the words echo, let the music rise, let the dreams take flight.

Miserere

Miserere and Misericordia to those who still believe the world can be remade, even when history insists otherwise.

And so let there be mercy and grace for all who seek it.

Mercy to the deserving, and even more to those who are not.

John Ricciardi

Conclusion

Empty Words When Pain Arrives

Having talked, throughout the book, about various behaviors of world leaders and the general public, I want to conclude by saying that normally most individuals use borrowed slogans like "life is short" (most common), "be happy", "don't worry", "God bless". These rhetorical slogans are quickly suggested and advised to those who have been victimized.

When suffering knocks on our own door, those same words collapse, we become nervous and unstable. The rhetoric we offer so freely proves hollow when we are the ones in pain. *Miserere* for the ease with which we speak. *Misericordia*, for the silence we must learn to hold.

The Paradox of Platitudes

In moments of others' suffering, individuals often resort to rhetorical platitudes, as a means of offering comfort. These expressions, while well-intentioned, often lack depth and fail to engage with the complexity of trauma. Yet, when the same individuals become victims themselves, their emotional stability falters. The slogans they once offered prove insufficient, revealing a disconnect between intellectualized empathy and embodied experience.

The paradox invites a deeper reflection: it is easy to throw around feel-good slogans when someone else is hurting, but when pain hits home, those same people fall apart.

Suddenly, the advice dries up, suddenly the slogans sound fake. Maybe it's time we sit with the discomfort (ours and theirs) and stop hiding behind empty words.

Our Common Humanity

We are all human beings. To manifest superiority or strive to emulate others is not only irrelevant but it is also a sign of immaturity.

Regardless of gender, color, race or background, our blood runs the same shade, red, and in the end we all arrive at the same destination.

We are all humans. To claim superiority, to imitate, to divide are all distractions from truth.

Gender, color, background, wealth, poverty do not change the fact that our blood is the color red and in the end we all return to the same place.

So why all the conflicts?

Let us all live to the best of our capacities and let others live as best as they possibly can.

Miserere and Misericordia for the pride we carry, for the pain we share and for the illusions we chase.

John Ricciardi

Epilogue

The protests faded, the regimes collapsed, the dreamers were buried beneath bureaucracy and dust.

And still the world spins, still the powerful forget, still the songs are sung.

If you have read this far, you are either complicit or you are awake.

To the ones who remember, *Miserere* and *Misericordia*.

To the ones who dare to begin again, *Miserere* and *Misericordia*.

Mercy is not weakness, sorrow is not surrender. The world forgot this, we must not.

They learned nothing, not from the chants, the revolts, the songs. Power does not listen, but history does.

The past is not behind us, it is beneath us, layered in ash, protests and forgotten hymns. We walk on it daily, we just do not look down.

John Ricciardi

www.ingramcontent.com/pod-product-compliance
Lightning Source LLC
Chambersburg PA
CBHW060501030426
42337CB00015B/1689